These Are the Days of Elijah

Expositions on Elijah and Elisha
The Book of Kings

A Guide for Personal
and Group Bible Study

With Questions and Notes for Discussion

David E. Ross

In memory of Professor Ronald S. Wallace,
who more than any other revealed
how the Old Testament continually points to
and is completed only in
the New Testament.

Acknowledgments

𐕣

This book found its beginning in the midst of a renewal that was taking place in my personal life and the life of my family more than forty years ago. Having served as cross-cultural missionaries for a decade, we were enjoying a sabbatical rest by seeking to know God more intimately, with a strong desire to deepen our knowledge and understanding of the Word of God in order to be more effective in our ministry of discipling university students and young adults in the land we were serving, Korea.

I had the good fortune of taking graduate school courses under a well-known Scottish Bible interpreter, Professor Ronald S. Wallace. His course titled *Elijah and Elisha* captivated me. His ability to enter into the life and thinking of these two prophets and to reveal through them the heart of much of Jesus' teaching in the New Testament impressed me deeply. That was when I began to "live with these two prophets," who are the subject of this study. I am very thankful for having had the privilege of knowing Dr. Wallace and studying under him.

Two other men who have helped me to couple solid biblical exposition with deep spiritual experience are Dr. Earl W. Morey, international Bible teacher and evangelist, and Dr. Gary A. Parrett, former associate professor of educational ministries at Gordon-Conwell Theological Seminary and beloved mentor of many young pastors and teachers. I appreciate both these men greatly and thank God for their continuing excellence in service to the Church. Both men wrote kind endorsements for my earlier book on Bible meditation, *A Table Before Me* (Xulon Press, 2007).

My heartfelt thanks go to my father in-law, the late Dr. T. Layton Fraser, greatly loved and highly respected professor of biblical studies at Presbyterian College, Clinton, South Carolina. He taught me to let the Scriptures speak for themselves, without compromise.

I am grateful for the Rev. Soon Chung, pastor of University Presbyterian Church at UCLA, for writing the foreword, and for his wife, Esther, who along with Laura Greanias graciously did the proofreading for the final edition.

In addition, my special thanks go to my beloved wife of fifty-five years, who loves God and His Word, has pioneered several ministries with me and has offered much needed advice in writing this book; and to our three children—Debbie, David and Becky—and their loving families, who are always a blessing and strong support.

Lastly, I thank my community here at Pneuma Springs for the privilege of being partners in ministry together with them, and for the great joy they bring to our life. Also, I am grateful to our larger community, some in other parts of North America, and many in Northeast Asia and other areas of the world. We call this community the "Community of the Holy Fire."

Many thanks go to Heajoung Yang for translating this book into Korean. And thank you, the reader, for allowing this small Bible study book to lead you into the exciting world of Elijah and Elisha.

Foreword

I am honored to write on behalf of David Ross, a man I truly respect and love. I met David Ross in 1985 while I was still in seminary, and have thus far learned a great deal from his excellent counsel and honest lifestyle. I genuinely cherish our relationship. He has not only had a monumental impact on my life as a mentor and teacher, but also as a dear friend. Consequently, it will come as no surprise that I readily agreed to write a foreword for his work.

As I progressed through the book, I was deeply struck by David's wonderful insight, knowledge and discernment. His experience in young adult ministry has developed his wisdom and perception and, as a result, allows him to effectively engage the reader while appealing to practicality. Moreover, he skillfully weaves together biblical knowledge and applicable truths, ultimately leading his audience to eye-opening conclusions. Accordingly, I have no doubt that David's work will intrigue readers as well as further their understanding.

The book's title, *These Are the Days of Elijah*, is in reference to a special day when God will require Christians to boldly speak the truth in a godless society, just as He commanded Elijah to urge Israel to stop worshiping Baal and turn back to Him. In their wealth and comfort, the

Israelites had forgotten their covenant with God. Similarly, many people today have turned away from God and become hostile to His message of love. It is amid this adversity that David challenges us to bring the hope of Jesus to the world. After all, as Christians, we are called to stand firm on the word of God, proclaim truth and participate with Jesus to destroy the works of the devil (1 John 3:8), just as Elijah was called to do ages ago.

Unfortunately, in the face of adversity, it is often easy to become passive; we tend to keep silent and appease people rather than strive to follow in God's footsteps. Nonetheless, we must remember that Christianity is a call to be a light and salt to society. We should not only speak the truth, but also live it out. This is something David has done throughout his entire life, and I am a witness to his living testimony. In fact, I am constantly learning from his example on how to live out the Christian life. As such, I am confident that *These Are the Days of Elijah* will prove to be more than merely a good read—it will prove to be extremely valuable, especially for those who wish to mature in their walk with the Lord.

> Rev. Dr. Soon Chung
> Head Pastor
> University Presbyterian Church
> UCLA Presbyterian Chaplain

Introduction

"*These* are the days of Elijah, declaring the Word of the Lord!" The Irish songwriter Robin Mark wrote this popular song in 1994 just after the Rwandan civil war tragedy that claimed one million lives, and also when the cease-fires in Northern Ireland were declared. In prayer, God assured him that He was very much in control and that "the days we were living in were special times when He would require Christians to be filled with integrity and to stand up for Him just as Elijah did, particularly with the prophets of Baal."[1]

Yes, modern-day "prophets of Baal" still assail the Church of the Living God. Just as they sought to destroy the family system in ancient Israel by destroying the minds of young children, just as they attempted to annihilate the community of believers by killing or otherwise attempting to silence God's appointed leaders, and just as they mocked God and tried to relegate Him to Israel's past history without any relevance to the everyday life of that present age, so they continue to do the same today.

But we do not despair, because we know the end of world history, which is God's great story of salvation! Jesus will return to judge the living and the dead! Satan and his evil powers, including the prophets of Baal and all other anti-God forces, will be destroyed forever. (Revelation 22:12-13) Already, God has highly exalted Jesus Christ *". . . and bestowed on Him the name that is above every name, so that at the name of Jesus every knee should bow, in heaven and on earth and under the earth, and every tongue confess that Jesus Christ is Lord, to the glory of God the Father."* (Philippians 2:9-11)

Jesus identified John the Baptist as the "Elijah" who had come *"to restore all things. . . by turning the hearts of the fathers to their children and the hearts of the children to their fathers, and the disobedient to the wisdom of the just, to make ready for the Lord a people prepared."* (Malachi 4:5-6; Matthew 17:10-12; Luke 1:16-17)

The purpose of this book is to "make ready for the Lord a people prepared." The full restoration of God's people will take place only when Jesus Christ returns again in glory. Until that time we must take our stand upon the Word of God, with full confidence in that eternal and unchanging Word. We must cling to the power of God through prayer and be obedient to the Holy Spirit, as Elijah and Elisha teach us to do. We will rediscover our roots of faith by examining the lives of these two prophets who knew the true source of their power.

Dr. Ronald S. Wallace, when he was teaching at Columbia Theological Seminary in Decatur, Georgia, first introduced me to these two prophets and taught me the centrality of Jesus Christ through these two vessels of clay. For forty years I have lived with these two prophets. Now it is time to tell their story. If we, as vessels of clay that are easily broken, submit wholly to the Lord as these two men did, we will also see transformation in our own nations and in the world.

David E. Ross
Pneuma Springs, 2012

"Long have I known that your instructions were laid down to last forever." (NJB)
Psalm 119:152

God's Word Remains

No shadow cast by turning,
No dimming as time goes by,
God's Word remains unchanging
While man's best ideas die.

Long have I known Your Word is true,
Your promises to me like gold,
Forever will they dawn anew
As years go by and time grows old.

Poems from Psalm 119
David E. Ross

Contents

Chapter One

Sent by the Living God
1 Kings 16:29-17:1

❧✠❧

" *As the Lord, the God of Israel, lives, before whom I stand...*" With these words, Elijah makes his first appearance at the time of Israel's greatest national crisis. King Ahab, who did more evil than all the kings before him, made matters worse by marrying Jezebel, daughter of the king of Sidon, whose religion was Baal worship.

Ahab may have thought that he could change her, but instead she changed him. King Ahab began to worship Baal rather than the true God. Jezebel brought hundreds of priests from her homeland and even set up altars to Baal in the temple of the living God. Although it was true that many Israelites had been practicing a form of Baal worship as a "hidden superstition" for a long time, Baal worship now became an openly militant force threatening to destroy the very fabric of Israel's life, its religious and moral traditions.

Baal was a Canaanite fertility cult, and Baal was considered to be the god of fertility and vegetation and of all things pertaining to the earth. The Baal prophets did what cults seek to do today: they targeted young people. They began to teach the youth to call on the name of Baal, just as they had been taught by their parents to call on the name of the Lord.

We may think we are listening to cult leaders today when we hear what they taught. They taught that Baal had been the true god of Canaan long before Israel had entered the land, and that Abraham and Moses brought in a foreign religion. They taught that the Lord God was the God of their past, having brought them out of Egypt. But Baal was the god of their present everyday life. Baal was the god who would give them good offspring of babies and cattle and abundant crops. Their teaching was that Baal was powerful to bless them in their present lives, for fertility in their fields and homes.

So Baal worship became extremely popular in Israel. They still worshiped God in a formalistic way, but they also worshiped Baal for their everyday needs. Jezebel's methods were ruthless as she determined to spread the religion of Baal throughout Israel. She murdered many priests of God and forced the others into hiding.

What was the result? Not much resistance! People did not seem to care that their freedom and their faith were being threatened; to them it was no cause for alarm. The reason? Trade was good; money was flowing into Israel from Tyre and Sidon; there was economic security and no unemployment. So what did it matter if the priests were killed or the truth suppressed? "God was dead." The people were comfortable.

What is the lesson for 21st-century Christians? "All the blessings that God gives to a nation in one generation can be quickly forfeited by succeeding generations if they do not value fully their heritage of liberty, or if they compromise with evil!"[2]

As the Lord God of Israel lives. . .

Enter Elijah! "The Lord God lives!" was the mark of his ministry. (1 Kings 17:1) He was a single-minded, "God-conscious" man of God with a great sense of mission. Where did he come from? Where did he get his religious training? What seminary did he graduate from? How did he receive his calling to be a prophet? We know as little about him as King Ahab knew. His appearance was sudden, his origins unknown.

Here is a word of comfort. When great movements of evil seem to be overtaking the world and many people begin to follow them, when the church appears to be so weak that the world easily overcomes it and attempts to make it irrelevant, we need not despair. God always works in His own mysterious ways. God works underground! God does not work only through famous preachers and leaders. He can raise His men and women from nowhere. (1 Corinthians 1:26-29) Our situation is never hopeless. God has His own people prepared, and He is Lord of all situations in our lives and ruler of nations. King Ahab thought God was dead, and all the people wondered. But one man knew better.

Elijah's life was marked by a cunning simplicity, which was a deliberate part of his plan and strategy. He probably looked like a hippie from the 1960's; everyone was amused at him. All he said was, *"As the Lord, the God of Israel, lives, before whom I stand, there shall be neither dew nor rain these years, except by my word."* But all this time his strategy was to quietly strike at the heart of Baal worship. Fertility—good crops, much fruit—made Baal what he was. Elijah was creating an atmosphere in which he could mock Baal. No rain meant no harvest. God sent a famine. Does He sometimes not do the same today to get our attention? Perhaps we are not so much like Elijah as we think but rather like Baal worshipers, seeking God's blessings rather than His will.

The supreme mark of Elijah's life was that he was willing to stake his life on God's unchanging Word— *"except by my word"*! He heard from the Lord and spoke out the Word of the Lord, not his own word. He interpreted the famine as being the judgment of God on a rebellious people and a call to repentance. This word would throw him into a life-or-death struggle against Ahab, Jezebel and all the rest of Israel. But he stood firm in his belief that God would honor his plan and words and prayers, because they came from God Himself. The result was that it did not rain. (James 5:17) The lack of rain and resulting famine showed that it was the Lord, not Baal, who gave them their fruitfulness. The God of Israel was stronger than the idol Baal.

Elijah had no alternative other than to trust God and obey Him completely. His life's motto might have been God's words in 1 Samuel 2:30: *"For those who honor Me I will honor, and those who despise Me shall be lightly esteemed."* Elijah believed in the living God who stands behind His living Word. He was willing to wrestle with God for his nation, using God's own Word as his weapon. God's Word became Elijah's word. In this he was a foreshadowing of Jesus Christ, the one Man whose word was *always* God's word. Jesus said later that *"if you abide in Me, and My words abide in you, ask whatever you wish, and it will be done for you."* (John 15:7) After raising Lazarus from the dead, Jesus said, *"Did I not tell you that if you believed you would see the glory of God?"* (John 11:40)

All of us will go into places where there is Baal or another idol like him. We will encounter situations where evil seems to be destroying all that is good, or where Satan threatens to destroy the Church. We must prepare ourselves to meet these situations by asking ourselves two questions: First, can we pray like Elijah? Second, can we challenge God on the basis of His Word? We must believe that behind our words stands the full authority of the living God.

We live in an age when we must expect a miracle from God, for only a miracle can save nations from destruction, free suffering Christians from Satan's plans to murder them, and restore the glory of God to His Church. This miracle will take place when we stake our lives on the Word of God and speak out to the world as Elijah did, "Thus says the Lord." The miracle will be the coming of the Holy Spirit to once again work His miracles of love and healing, to bring life to a dying world.

We must have the same conviction that burned in Elijah's heart, that when we base our lives on the Word of God, our words will carry the full authority and power of God for the transformation of the world.

Lord, may Your Kingdom come, your will be done on earth, through us, servants of Your Word.

Questions for Further Thought and Discussion
Please read 1 Kings 16:29-17:1
before answering these questions.

1. The people of Elijah's day were willing to compromise God's truth for the sake of a comfortable life. Do you think this is happening today? If so, how are we compromising the truth of the Gospel? What can we do about it?

2. When God speaks, what He commands happens. Elijah staked his life on the Word of God, and when he spoke God acted. When we read God's Word, or when we hear the Word of God, do we expect anything to happen? If so, what?

3. Ask yourself the following question: "Do I consider myself a praying Christian? Can I pray like Elijah, who was not a superman but simply a man like me, challenging God on the basis of His Word?"

Notes

The Purpose of Miracles in the Bible

A miracle has been defined as "an event in which the hand of God, which is always there, can be more clearly traced than at other times." (Dibelius) St. Thomas Aquinas (c. 1225 – 74) said, "Those happenings that are properly called miraculous are done by divine agency outside the commonly observed order of things."

However we may describe miracles, the Bible is full of them. And God continues to work miracles today.

The Old Testament contains fewer miracles than the New Testament. They occurred mainly during the time of the Exodus and the wilderness journeys of God's people, or during the times of nation building, as in the ministry of Elijah and Elisha, or of Joshua. Nevertheless they occurred throughout the Old Testament. But the New Testament abounds in the miraculous. John the Apostle says of Jesus Christ that He did many other miracles that are not contained in the Gospels.

Another word used for miracles in the Bible is "signs." Miracles are signs that point to the truth of God in Jesus Christ. Just as miracles authenticated the words of the Old Testament prophets, so they authenticated the message of the apostles in the New Testament. Through miracles "God not only demonstrates His presence and power but also illuminates His purpose and the nature of His will and message."[3]

Pray that God will open your eyes to see the miracles He is performing all around you, and that He will use your faith to continue to work miracles for the advancement of the Kingdom of God.

Chapter Two

Detachment and Involvement
1 Kings 17:2-9

彡器ゝ

*E*lijah received no support from anyone on the day he took his stand on the Word of God. There was no one who could give him guidance or direction, and there was no one who would provide for his daily needs. Elijah learned very early that his home was in God. God alone was his security, and he must rely on God alone for all his needs. He could confess with the psalmist, *"The Lord is my shepherd, I shall not want."* (Psalm 23:1)

Detachment and involvement

God prepared Elijah by teaching him one of the basic principles of ministry: detachment and involvement. The Word of the Lord came to Elijah: *"Depart from here and hide yourself."* But later the Lord told him, *"Go, show yourself to Ahab."* (1 Kings 18:1) Throughout his ministry, Elijah was at times hidden and at other times bold in confronting the adversaries of God. He learned the principle of abiding. Centuries before the coming of Jesus Christ, the Holy Spirit taught Elijah the truth of John 15:5: *"I am* the vine; you are the branches. Whoever abides in Me and I in him, he it is that bears much fruit, for apart from Me you can do nothing."

Hiddenness

The Lord placed Elijah in hiding before He allowed him to begin his public ministry. This pattern of hiddenness is found throughout the Bible: Jesus was hidden for nearly thirty years before His public ministry; Joseph was hidden for thirteen years before God used him to save Egypt and other nations from famine; God hid Moses for forty years in the wilderness to prepare him for the great task of the exodus; Paul could not begin his powerful ministry until he had spent three years in hiddenness.

We are blessed to serve a God who welcomes us into His "hiding place" during times of trouble, fear, temptation or indecision. However, today we often avoid God's Spirit who wants to "hide" us for periods of time during our ministry. And by so doing we become burned out, begin to feel estranged from God and other co-workers and lose the strength and courage we need to serve a hostile world.

Yet we live in the world as servants. Jesus was the "Suffering Servant" to whom the prophet Isaiah pointed. A mark of his life was hiddenness. *"In the shadow of His hand He hid me,"* says the Lord's Servant. (Isaiah 49:2) We also are suffering servants in ministry with Jesus. We must at times be detached from ministry. Elijah must have been eager to quickly begin his spiritual warfare with the wicked prophets of Baal. But he soon found himself not only "under the Word of God," but also "under the providence of God." Why then does God sometimes hide the missionaries He tells to go into all the world and proclaim the Gospel of the Kingdom?

28

He hides us at times to protect us from harm, or to comfort us in trouble. He hides us when He knows that our character is not fully developed to be able to minister in His Spirit, as He did with Joseph in Egypt. During his hidden years, Joseph learned humility, forgiveness, generosity and great wisdom that he could have learned no other way. God hides us at times to keep us from undue popularity that could destroy God's work, from busyness, from striving to please others by hard work, or to protect us from craving acknowledgment. He also hides us for deep, abiding, intimate fellowship with Him. *"Keep me as the apple of Your eye; hide me in the shelter of Your wings."* (Psalm 17:8) He hides us to speak to us when we do not listen to Him in our daily life, just as He did to Hosea's wife Gomer: *"Therefore, behold, I will allure her, and bring her into the wilderness, and speak tenderly to her."* (Hosea 2:14) Above all, God hides us to make us ready to move with Him in His timing, for the maximum way He wants to use us.

God sometimes hides nations, like North Korea or Burma. He hides churches, especially in persecuted nations, to protect them and also to prepare them to be His instruments to renew their nations. Often the longer the preparation, the greater the work God does through His servants.

Flow of ministry

We must learn the balance, or the flow of ministry. We go out in faith, boldly, with the authority that Christ has given us. We trust Him to work miracles and to convey His saving grace to others through our ministry. But then we come back home again, into the presence of the Lord. We separate ourselves from the world in order to hear God's Word as He speaks to us in intimacy. We must remember that our home is in *the presence of God,* not in the world. When our family was forced to abruptly leave Korea in 1986, where we had served for twenty-five years, we felt that our ministry had come to an end. But when I returned to the mountain retreat where we had been commissioned long ago for missionary service and climbed the mountain where I had met God and received His anointing for ministry, God spoke to me, saying, "This is your home, My son, here in My presence, resting in My love. Your ministry is not to perform great deeds in My name, but rather to love Me as I love you, and to trust Me to use you for My glory. You do not need to do anything for Me; I will do My work through you when I send you out to minister to a broken, hurting world." Immediately I remembered God's Word to Israel through the prophet Hosea: *"From Me comes your fruit."* (Hosea 14:8)

I was forced to relinquish the ministry that had become my idol. It was not my decision to detach myself from the work that I was doing; it was God's. He took me into hiding because I had not yet learned the lesson of *detachment and engagement.* I had not learned that my home was not in my ministry but was in God. I thank God for teaching me, through failure, the most important lesson of my missionary life: to abide in Christ is the secret of effective ministry. Just as to be hidden and sustained by God was for Elijah the sign he needed from God at this time in his life, so I discovered that God was preparing me for the battles ahead.

"Hide yourself" was spoken not only to Elijah but also to all servants of the Lord. The Holy Spirit hid the prophet Ezekiel by taking him directly into heaven through a spectacular vision. It was a vision of the glory of God and His judgment on His people, which Ezekiel faithfully revealed to his people in exile. From time to time Jesus hid Himself away from the crowds in order to be with His

Father. When Jesus saw that His disciples were becoming too immersed in their work and anxious in spirit, He told them to come aside and rest a while with Him. Is it not true that if we would learn to be separate from the world in our spirits, we might be able to more clearly discern God's Word for the world and be strengthened to proclaim that Word with more boldness?

The Lord's Supper, or Eucharist, is where we can rediscover our hiddenness in Christ. The Early Church celebrated the Lord's Supper often, probably daily, and in so doing learned that their home was in God, and that from this home they could go out to witness and serve and then return home to the perfect peace of Christ. Perhaps we should consider the importance of participating in the Supper of our Lord more frequently than just once a month, or several times a year. Even John Calvin desired that his churches would celebrate Holy Communion weekly. We may do better to celebrate it daily, to maintain our hiddenness with the Lord.

Jesus called the twelve "so that they *might be with Him* and He *might send them out to preach.*" (Mark 3:14) They learned that whatever their circumstances might be, they could always count on the protection of the Lord. They learned that their life was hidden with Christ in God. (Colossians 3:3) But then God "sent them out to preach."

God did not permit Elijah to remain hidden in sheltered seclusion by the brook Cherith. After a while He told him to rise and go to Zarephath and minister to a widow in need. Elijah had to go into the broken world and learn to share the pain of those who experienced hardship and hopelessness. Neither did Ezekiel remain in the intimate place of glory forever, separated from his people. Immediately after the vision, God sent him back to Tel-abib to live among his people. He wrote, *"I sat there overwhelmed among them seven days."* (Ezekiel 3:15)

Spirituality flows outward

We must be careful not to allow ourselves to fall into the trap of seeking spiritual enrichment and growth only for ourselves and thus become separated from the world. When Dr. Wallace used to teach us about Elijah and Elisha, he would say over and over again that the Christian life is not a matter of storing up accumulated resources. We must not spend too much time trying to develop our devotional life at the expense of witnessing to people whom God sends to us. God does not give us the spiritual disciplines as a selfish "spiritual luxury." That is not God's way. Spirituality flows outward, not inward. We go in Jesus' name to sit with people who are heartbroken, who are suffering and dying. As we go, God's grace is sufficient for all our needs. Jesus enjoyed the presence of God more than any man. Yet He also "sat among men and bore their sufferings and sorrows as no other prophet ever did."[4] He endured hunger and thirst and bore the sins of the whole world upon Himself on the cross.

Here is the secret of continual renewal, the secret of spiritual authority, and the secret of power in ministry. When we learn this secret, the world will recognize that even though we are common, ordinary men and women, we *have been with Jesus!* (Acts 4:13)

Questions for Further Thought and Discussion
Please read 1 Kings 17:2-9
before answering these questions.

1. We have seen examples of people whom God has "hidden." Have you ever experienced being hidden by God? What did God do for you during that time? What were some things you learned?

2. Jesus called His disciples that they might be with Him and that He might send them out to proclaim the Gospel. (Mark 3:14) God did not allow Elijah to remain hidden by the brook Cherith. After a time He sent him out to impart God's life to a suffering world. What did you learn in this lesson about "detachment" from the world to be with Christ, in order to be "involved" in the world to serve people?

3. Can people sense from your involvement in the world that you have "been with Jesus?" Would you say that you have a balanced life between "going out" to serve the world and "coming back home" to be in Jesus' presence?

Notes

Solitude

The essence of the spiritual life is to walk with the Lord, led and empowered by the Holy Spirit. (See David E. Ross, *A Table Before Me: The Meditating Christian*, p. 81ff.) To consciously seek to be in the presence of the Lord through prayer and meditation on God's Word, to confess that I desire to be with Him just as He desires to be with me, is the beginning of our spiritual journey. This is the essence of *solitude*. It means to be "alone with God," to live our lives in the presence of the One who knows and loves us completely, with the one goal of pleasing Him.

As Christians, we seek to develop a lifestyle of solitude. In order to make this possible, we must set aside a daily time in our busy schedules to be "alone with the Lord."

The direction of solitude is not flowing inward, deeper and deeper into ourselves. Rather, solitude flows outward, into the world. A meditator, or a contemplative, is not a saint who must separate himself from the world, protected from the affairs of daily life so as not to lose his spirituality. No, we walk with Christ into the marketplace. We walk into the broken world with the One who heals all brokenness.

Solitude, then, has two important marks: *detachment* and *involvement* (or *engagement*). We are in solitude with the Lord both when we come apart from our work and activity to be with Him and to enjoy communion with Him, and also when we walk out into the world with Christ to minister with Him to those in sorrow and grief. Whether we come apart from the world through detachment or go out into the world through involvement with people, we remain in solitude with Christ. Our great desire is to participate with God in the healing of the nations.

Chapter Three

Direct and Indirect Provision
1 Kings 17:2-24

☙ ❦ ❧

*G*od prepares us for ministry by teaching us the flow of ministry. At times He calls us to be detached from outward ministry, hidden from the people to whom we minister. At other times He leads us to be with people, opening ourselves to them, becoming vulnerable and involved in their lives. We must know this rhythm and live it, being sensitive to the leading of the Spirit.

But there is another way He equips us, and that is by providing for all our needs so that we can serve Him freely and be generous in meeting the needs of others. He teaches us to rely on Him alone for all our needs, whether the needs are spiritual, emotional, physical or material. He alone is our source. God caused water to come out of the rock; He fed His people with manna in the wilderness. Is He not the same today? All that we need for life and ministry is provided by our Shepherd.

Direct and indirect provision

The two ways God provided for Elijah were by direct means and indirect means. God first provided Elijah's needs directly, by giving him water to drink from the brook Cherith and by using ravens to feed him. Then He provided for him indirectly, through the widow of Zarephath.

Where did the ravens get the bread and meat to feed Elijah twice a day? The famine was growing more severe throughout the land, and good food was scarce. There was one place, however, where food was never scarce: the king's table. Just as in poor nations today where many people are starving and the leaders continue to live in luxury, so it was in the days of Elijah. Perhaps the ravens got the food from King Ahab's table and fed Elijah royally.

Elijah needed this sign from God as he was beginning his ministry. God would take care of him! Ultimately he knew that he must not depend on people for his needs, but only on God. Hudson Taylor knew this spiritual truth. His friends criticized him for planning to take his three children deep into the interior of China, where no Western missionary had gone before and where he could not get supplies to feed them properly. His reply was that he himself, as a father, knew his children's needs, and did not God the Father know even better all the needs that his children would have? Hudson Taylor went on to raise up more than five thousand missionaries who knew how to trust God for all their needs.

"After a while the brook dried up. . ." God uses many ways to provide for His people, but no one method is permanent. No one method is more spiritual than other methods. We must learn to put our absolute trust in God alone, and not in the methods or principles He uses. His

methods are changeable; only God is permanent. His Word is permanent.

"I have commanded a widow there to feed you. . ." God fed him *directly*, through the ravens, to teach him to trust Him when there was no human to help him. Then He fed him *indirectly* through another person. Elijah must have been shocked when he discovered that the person God had prepared to minister to him was near death and had only enough food to prepare one last meal for her son before he died. It must have been hard for him to believe that this poor woman could be God's "ministering angel" to him. The widow had received no vision that a prophet would come, so she also must have been shocked when Elijah asked her for her last supply of food. God did not tell Elijah to go to this poverty-stricken widow and ask for only one meal. He told him to go and live there!

The truth is that they both needed each other. Elijah needed the widow to feed him and to help him truly understand how the people to whom God was sending him were suffering; she needed Elijah to save her life and restore her hope. Later, in the New Testament, Jesus preached a sermon in Capernaum about this story of Elijah and the widow, and His emphasis was that this poor woman was the most unlikely person in all the land to minister to Elijah. She was not even an Israelite, but rather lived in Sidon of Phoenicia where the famine had also spread. Nevertheless, she obeyed "according to the word of Elijah." Then her own needs were provided for "according to the Word of the Lord." *"The bowl of flour was not exhausted nor did the jar of oil become empty, according to the Word of the Lord."* (1 Kings 17:16)

Mother Teresa spoke often about the beauty and generosity of the poor who surrounded her. She said many times that they ministered to her far more than she ministered to them. She said that God often surrounds us by poor, broken and destitute people in order to minister to our needs through them. We go to serve them, but they actually minister to us! The cause of world evangelization is often furthered not so much by rich churches and wealthy Christians as it is by poor and needy people who know the Gospel and live according to it with a spirit of generosity. Paul described the Macedonian churches, chief among them the Philippians, this way: *"For in a severe test of affliction, their abundance of joy and their extreme poverty have overflowed in a wealth of generosity on their part."* (2 Corinthians 8:2)

Living by faith

What does it mean to "live by faith" in terms of finances? We are not speaking only about missionaries who go to foreign lands and live by faith, but also about all Christians regardless of where they live or what kind of jobs they might have—or not have. All of God's people must live by faith, for there is no other way to please God! (Hebrews 11:6) Some people live by faith without any visible or known means of support. God provides for their needs. Others live by faith who receive a salary from a company but who know that all things belong to God and they have no ownership over their money, their property or belongings. God also provides for their needs.

"Living by faith" means to wake up each morning praising God and thanking Him for the air He gives us to breathe, and for giving us another day of life to glorify His name. It means to give ownership of all that we have to God and allow Him to rule over our finances, to put all that we have at His disposal. Living by faith means to place everything I am and all that I have in the hands of God, for Him to use for His glory. It means to live a life of generosity by obeying the Holy Spirit when He tells us to give to others. It means to put money in the bank and save it if He reveals to us the purpose for which it should be saved. Or it could mean to draw money out of the bank and give it to whomever He chooses. It means to trust God alone for all our needs, but to be thankful and humble when He directs another person to provide for our needs. Here we find two things essential to living by faith: first, intimacy with God, as a lifestyle and also as a daily discipline through His Word; second, a spirit of generosity that enables us to give with joy, even out of our poverty.

Will you be willing to trust God to this level, to follow Him totally? If so, you are about to begin an exciting journey with the Lord. And God will use your life to bless many people, even to bless nations!

Dealing with a crisis

Elijah stayed at the widow's house, blessed by God's daily miracles of grace and mercy. He helped raise her son, and we can imagine that he taught him the ways of a true disciple of the Lord. But a crisis suddenly arose with the sudden death of the son. The widow began to question all that Elijah had done. She remembered that before Elijah came on the scene there had been prosperity in Israel, even though it came through Baal worship. She forgot the miracle that God had performed for her. Was He a God of mercy? Or was He a God of judgment? Her inner conflict must have been great.

Are we not like both Elijah and this widow? We are surrounded by many signs of God's grace and love that give us courage. Yet there are other signs that cause us to question God's goodness and providence. Satan's power in the world is still strong; the innocent suffer and even die. How could Elijah reconcile the great miracle he had experienced with this great tragedy? Here we see the humanity of Elijah; he was a man just like ourselves. Our faith is tested, sometimes daily, and we must make a decision to trust God even when we cry out to Him, *"I believe; help my unbelief!"* (Mark 9:24)

We have seen, through this story, two signs. God showed Elijah how much He loved and cared for him by feeding him miraculously. Then God showed a sign of His love for the widow and her son by keeping them alive and providing for their welfare. But a third sign followed, the sign of resurrection! Elijah acted on his faith and prayed; the child came back to life again! Three resurrections actually took place: Elijah's own resurrection when God fed him miraculously; the widow's resurrection when she faced death; and the son's resurrection from death. This story points to the central event in the history of mankind. The resurrection of Jesus Christ from the dead is God's final answer to Satan's attacks, to the world's disbelief, and to the doubts of God's people.

God used these three signs to prepare Elijah for even greater warfare to revive a dying nation. Notice how Elijah dealt with the problem. He immediately prayed with full trust in the God of resurrection. He prayed in secret. He did not find it necessary to broadcast all the miracles of God. The miracle took place through Elijah's quiet abiding in God and his trust in the Word of God.

These miracles prepared Elijah for the biggest test of his life: his encounter with the prophets of Baal on Mount Carmel to save his nation. They also prepared the widow. She was only one seemingly insignificant person, but later she became a symbol of the whole nation. Her response to God's saving love was a sign that Israel would come to believe in the living God through the great miracle to be manifested on Mount Carmel.

Questions for Further Thought and Discussion
Please read 1 Kings 17:2-24
before answering these questions.

1. Becoming a Christian involves turning over the owner-ship of our lives and possessions to God, for Him to use as He pleases. This means that *all* Christians must *live by faith,* whether it is by trusting God with no human source of income or by trusting God with an expected salary. At different seasons in our lives, God may lead us to live by one method, and another time He may lead us in a dif-ferent direction. No one financial method of living is the only absolute way, nor is any method permanent. God alone is the source of all we have, and He may change His method of supplying. Living by faith requires trans-ferring all ownership over to God, seeking intimacy with Him and practicing generosity. Are you committed to living by faith? If so, what changes will this require in your lifestyle?

2. When God wanted to provide for Elijah and encourage him, He sent him to a poverty-stricken foreigner whom Elijah did not know. Why do you think God sent him to this woman? Mother Teresa said that the poor ministered to her needs in wonderful ways. What does this say about our needs today?

3. Note the persistence of both Elijah and the widow when the widow's son died. Both of them were angry with God and refused to give up until God raised the son from the dead. Read the parable of the persistent widow in Luke 18:1-8. What can we learn from this?

Notes

Intimacy with God and Generosity

There are instances when God calls a person to a specific work that requires the person to give up everything and trust God alone for all needs. The great missionaries Hudson Taylor, William Carey, George Mueller and many others lived this way. God provided for all their needs so completely that George Mueller was able to feed thousands of orphans daily, although he had no regular income or donors; Hudson Taylor was able to raise up five thousand missionaries who would live as he lived, trusting God alone for their finances. When God calls a person to live in this way, He often gives them the *gift* of faith (1 Corinthians 12:7-11). This enables them to trust God in situations where others cannot. Such people do not have to use all their energies in fund raising. Rather they concentrate on *intimacy with God* and living lives that are pleasing to Him.

The common mark of such persons is *generosity.* Read through 2 Corinthians chapters eight and nine and take note of the spirit of the churches of Macedonia, who in a *severe test of affliction* displayed *abundance of joy,* and in *extreme poverty "overflowed in a wealth of generosity"*! Notice God's promises as you read through these two chapters. Note also how the Body of Christ was built up through the churches of Macedonia.

Chapter Four

The Hidden Church
1 Kings 18:1-16

*lijah's preparation continued. He must have wondered what was happening in the outside world. Three years had passed, and nothing had changed. God kept him hidden, in silence, and allowed him to do nothing to change the fate of his nation. God was doing with Elijah the same thing He later would do with His own Son, the Suffering Servant. Elijah, like Jesus, already had the Word of the Lord. God had made his mouth like a "sharp sword," yet He hid him in the shadow of His hand. He made him a "polished arrow" so that God's Word would go far and wide throughout the land, yet God hid him away in His quiver. (Isaiah 49:2)

The importance of timing

Timing was the heart of Elijah's ministry, just as it is for us today. All times are in God's hands, and Elijah could do nothing and speak nothing until God told him that the time for action had come. The right thing done in God's right timing will have powerful results. Joseph waited thirteen years, Moses forty years. The prophets of the Old Testament prophesied about the coming of the Messiah, but it was a long time after they had grown weary in watching and waiting that He sent His Son. Yet the timing was perfect! *"When the fullness of time had come, God sent forth His Son."* (Galatians 4:4) Even after He entered the world, Jesus waited thirty years before beginning His ministry of salvation for the world. God alone knows the times and seasons, and He alone knows when to say, "Hide yourself, the time has not yet come." We must not grow weary in waiting; rather, we must trust God for His timing.

But God's time had now come. Elijah knew the rhythm of ministry, and he had waited in humility and patience. God spoke: *"Go, show yourself to Ahab."* The time had come to destroy the house of Ahab and remove its evil from God's people. We can best understand the situation by Jesus' teaching in the parable of the wheat and tares, in Matthew 13:24-30. Both grow together until the harvest; evil is mixed in with the good, the false with the true. But just as good wheat has to ripen for the harvest, so evil has to "ripen for judgment" before the harvest. To separate them too early is bad. In Israel, Jezebel had sown tares among the wheat; but now Baal was ripe for the harvest. God kept Elijah hidden for three years, because God knew Elijah would have been unprepared, and the circumstances would not be ready; Elijah would have been killed.

We must understand the courage of the man Elijah. Ahab had sworn to kill him because he held him accountable for all the troubles of Israel. His army searched for him everywhere but could not find him because God had hidden him. Elijah was alone; no one stood with him. But he resolutely obeyed God and went out to face Ahab, Jezebel, hundreds of Baal priests and a nation that neither understood nor accepted him. We can see in Elijah a foreshadowing of Jesus when He steadfastly set His face toward Jerusalem, to confront the powers of evil and to lay down His life on the cross.

But was Elijah truly alone? He stood alone, but were there no other believers among the nation of Israel who were concerned about the fate of their nation? Indeed there were; God later told Elijah that there was a large *hidden church! "Yet I will leave seven thousand in Israel, all the knees that have not bowed to Baal, and every mouth that has not kissed him."* (1 Kings 19:18) It is even possible that God may have led some of these hidden Christians to pray for Elijah.

Obadiah, the hidden believer

Elijah met one of the hidden believers. Obadiah "feared the Lord greatly" and was in a very influential position in Ahab's government. He lived in King Ahab's palace, at the very heart of Baal worship. Obadiah's continual presence in the king's palace was a miracle, just as great as Elijah's miracle that would be performed on Mount Carmel.

Ahab trusted Obadiah with the responsibility of his entire household, because God gave Obadiah favor in the king's sight. *"When a man's ways please the Lord, He makes even his enemies to be at peace with him."* (Proverbs 16:7) He was in charge of everything that belonged to Ahab. He had Ahab's "seal," so he could distribute food and other essential things as he wished. He used his position of influence to save lives. He regarded Elijah as his *master* and did all he could to protect other prophets by hiding and feeding one hundred prophets of the Lord! Elijah needed Obadiah, who was faithful to God and faithful to Elijah.

At the heart of the Church's mission to the world is the power of *Christian presence.* One does not have to be an ordained pastor or a professional missionary to do missions. The greatest witness to the world of the Lordship of Jesus Christ is a life lived for the glory of God without compromise. It is a life totally committed to Jesus Christ to be an instrument for world evangelization. It is a life made available to God, wherever we might be. We may be in the business world, or in education or the arts. But if we are committed to God, there is no limit to how He can use us for His glory, *right where we are!*

We find many "Obadiah-like" people in the Bible. Daniel did not compromise when he was in the court of the kings of Babylonia and Persia. Rather, he set his heart to fear the Lord and understand His ways. Naaman returned to his homeland as commander of the army of the king of Syria, but he had been healed by Elisha and this time he returned as a "hidden believer in God." The Apostle Paul closed his letter to the Philippians with the words, *"All the saints greet you, especially those of Caesar's household."* (Philippians 4:22)

The Hidden Church

So there was a Hidden Church in Elijah's day. And there is a Hidden Church today, in nearly every nation of the world. Among them are men and women, and even children, who live in the centers of power held by presidents, prime ministers, even dictators. Many of them are trusted by those in authority over them. These are God's people who are faithful to Him. He has hidden them for His great purposes among the nations of the world.

Today God is calling His intercessors to pray for the Hidden Church. Many people seek to help by providing food and other assistance to hidden Christians. But the

Hidden Church by definition is a church where there is no outside access. No one knows how many Christians would be in the Hidden Church in any given nation, and most people would have no contact with them. In most cases it is not possible to help them in tangible ways. But one thing we can do is intercede.

Yet most Christians are more eager to help in material ways than they are to pray. God wonders why Christians do not pray; He is actually shocked, according to the prophets. *"He saw that there was no man, and wondered that there was no one to intercede...."* (Isaiah 59:16) *"And I sought for a man among them who should build up the wall and stand in the breach before Me for the land, that I should not destroy it, but I found none."* (Ezekiel 22:30)

Missionaries have taken the Gospel to almost every nation of the world. The unreached people groups are being reached today, in one of the greatest periods of world missions the world has known. God has planted His Church in Iran, in Burma (Myanmar), in North Korea and among forgotten tribal groups and difficult-to-reach tribal peoples. Once the church flourished in North Korea, but now it is hidden. Yet as one walks along the banks of the Taedong River in Pyongyang, with its majestic weeping willow trees adorning its beautiful flowing waters, one stands in awe at the mysteries and wisdom of God who has planted His human trees of righteousness in that land, to bless the land and bring prosperity and peace to its people. How many Obadiahs are there waiting, listening to the Lord, ready to obey His will?

We must intercede for the Hidden Church. Pray that God may grant favor to these unseen Christians in ways that will bless their nations. Pray that they will be faithful in adversity. Pray for their health and the well-being of their families. Pray that God Himself will appear to them supernaturally to encourage and strengthen them, and to speak to them of the "great and mighty things that they do not know." (Jeremiah 33:3) Pray that they will be strengthened and be bold to be Christ's witnesses where they are.

Elijah's prayer ministry is available to all Christians. God has given us His Word, His treasure chest that enriches us each time we open it. He is ready to do the works He did through Christ, and even greater works, which are made possible by prayer. (John 14:12-14)

Questions for Further Thought and Discussion
Please read 1 Kings 18:1-16
before answering these questions.

1. Persecution of Christians is greater today than at any other time in history. One result is that many Christians are unknown even by other Christians in their own nation and hidden from the outside world. Perhaps there are many Obadiahs among them, whom God has placed in positions of influence among the nations. Others are nameless people who have no voice to be able to speak out concerning their condition. What do you think it means to be the "voice for the voiceless" in the world today? What are some ways we can help these persecuted, hidden Christians?

2. Consider some ways to intercede for the persecuted Christians. Ask God to share His heart with you for these "little people of God." Seek God for ways to participate in their suffering as we lift them up before the throne of God.

3. "Christian Presence" is a term used to denote Christians who may not have the right to assemble for worship, or to pray and read the Bible openly, but who nevertheless are witnesses for Christ by their very presence. How do you understand the importance of "Christian Presence" in the Suffering Church today?

Notes

The Hidden Church

When we speak of the "underground church" in difficult-access nations today, we actually are talking about the Hidden Church. It is scarcely visible, yet it is present. God has planted His "trees of righteousness"—people like Obadiah—in strategic places throughout these lands.

Often there are some churches that the various governments allow to be open in their capital cities. These churches are authentic churches when the Word of God is preached, and when Christians are able to praise God and celebrate the sacraments.

But the vast majority of Christians in these nations are not visible to government authorities or to visitors from outside the country. They are hidden, but they are not dead. On the contrary they are very much alive. As the Hidden Church, they continue to battle the forces of evil and remain victorious through the protection of God's Holy Spirit. Not only the Suffering Church, but also "the whole church," writes Thomas Merton, "is still passing out of Egypt." The Church "has been delivered from bondage to Pharaoh (the world, the devil, sin), is protected in her journey (through the wilderness) to the Promised Land and is finally admitted to the peace of perfect union with God in heaven."[5]

Merton loved the Psalms and spoke of them as our Bread of Heaven in the wilderness. For this reason the Psalms provide excellent material for prayer for those Christians living in ungodly nations, like those seven thousand believers in Elijah's day who had not bowed their knees to Baal. The greatest thing we can do for them is to pray for them and commit them to the Lord's loving care. Soon there will come a day when many of these "hidden Christians" will be able to arise and be used openly by God to serve Him as leaders of the churches God is restoring in nations ruled by totalitarian governments.

Chapter Five

Spiritual Warfare
2 Kings 18:17-46

ll Christians are engaged in spiritual warfare. Paul describes the type of war we wage: *"For we do not wrestle against flesh and blood, but against the rulers, against the authorities, against the cosmic powers over this present darkness, against the spiritual forces of evil in the heavenly places."* (Ephesians 6:12)

The outcome is clear, for us as it was with Elijah. When God called Elijah to confront Ahab, He was calling him to confront all the spiritual rulers and authorities, and all the cosmic powers of evil that were controlling Ahab and causing darkness in the land of Israel. Then He added, *". . . and I will send rain upon the earth."* The long years of famine would come to an end and God would once again restore life and fruitfulness to His people.

The troubler of Israel

The Hidden Church surrounded Elijah, but it was this one man God was calling to engage in open warfare. First he had to meet Ahab, who greeted him with the strange remark, *"Is it you, you troubler of Israel?"* Actually it was Ahab who was the troubler of Israel, because he had abandoned the commandments of the Lord and followed gods who were in reality "spiritual forces of evil in the heavenly places." Ancient Israel was the prime example of what happens to a nation that turns its back on the Word of God and follows false idols. This should be a warning to nations today, to the United States, to the nations of Europe, to South Korea, and to all other nations that are turning away from the one true God and worshiping false idols.

But why was Ahab troubled because of this one man? Perhaps he saw in Elijah what the ungodly Jews in Thessalonica saw in Paul and Silas when they said, *"These men who have turned the world upside down have come here also."* (Acts 17:6) Surely Ahab knew that his own world was about to be turned upside down when Elijah demanded a confrontation with the four hundred and fifty prophets of Baal and the four hundred prophets of Asherah.

Miracles point to a sign

Elijah's sermon was more important than his miracle. This is true of all the miracles in the New Testament as well as those that happen today. Miracles point to a sign. God continues to work miracles both to bless and teach His people. The sign is the truth found only in the Bible, the one authentic Word of God, that God alone is almighty, that He is the Lord of all nations and the ruler of the universe. All nations and all individuals are in His hands, and He alone directs the course of human history. Elijah performed the miracle to show the people the truth he proclaimed.

The danger of religious compromise

Elijah's sermon is summed up in one verse (1 Kings 18:21): *"How long will you go limping between two different opinions? If the Lord is God, follow Him; but if Baal, then follow him."* It was a call to decision. He told them that it was impossible to have "both. . . and;" they must choose "either. . . or." The people had chosen the Lord *and* Baal. They continued to worship the Lord as their "chief national God." But at the same time they welcomed Baal as the god of fertility and blessing in their homes; they built altars for him and bowed before him. They enjoyed an "inclusive" religion.

Many Christians in the Early Church were not that different; they worshiped Jesus Christ but at the same time they adopted rituals and practices from the pagan religions of the Roman Empire. Before we pass judgment on Israel or the early Christians, we should be aware that we do the same thing today. We enjoy Jesus Christ *and* all the material benefits that come from the world of mammon; we continue to follow Christ while priding ourselves on being inclusive and tolerant enough to accept other religions as another way to God.

This kind of religious compromise seemed good to the Jews of Elijah's day. It may seem good to many today. But God was not pleased; neither was Elijah. No one ever forgot his final challenge: *"How long will you go on limping between two different opinions?"* He was asking, "How long will you remain *spiritual cripples?"* Failure to decide for God alone cripples the soul. When the Apostle Paul faced a similar situation, he stated with conviction that the Christian faith can never be "both. . . and;" we always must choose. *"For I decided to know nothing among you except Jesus Christ and Him crucified."* (1 Corinthians 2:2) Today this is our message: the cross of Jesus Christ. Our task is to bring people to the cross and say, "You must choose Jesus Christ, crucified and raised again, in order to have eternal life."

The people must not have considered Elijah to be a good preacher. *"They did not answer him a word."* His preaching failed; now God had to speak for Himself and give witness to Elijah's words. God has done this throughout biblical history. The writer of Hebrews says that after people proclaimed God's great salvation, *"God also bore witness by signs and wonders and various miracles and by gifts of the Holy Spirit distributed according to His will."* (Hebrews 2:4) God must bring His fire!

Elijah and the false prophets

The stage was set: Elijah against eight hundred and fifty false prophets. Elijah threw out the challenge: *"You call upon the name of your god, and I will call upon the name of the Lord, and the God who answers by fire, he is God."*

God has promised to bring this fire from heaven to everyone today who confesses Jesus Christ as Lord and witnesses to His cross and resurrection. John the Baptist said, *"I baptize you with water for repentance, but He who is coming. . . will baptize you with the Holy Spirit and fire."* (Matthew 3:11) This promise was fulfilled when the Holy Spirit fell on the disciples at Pentecost. The fire of the Holy Spirit! Burning away the sins of rebellion and indecision, setting our hearts on fire for the Word of God, empowering us to be God's witnesses, and uniting us in the warmth of His love to become one so that the world might believe!

The contrast between Elijah and the false prophets could not have been greater. The prophets of Baal were desperate; their behavior was strained, because they were trying to produce their own fire. Elijah, on the other hand, was calm and confident, because he had already taken his stand on the unchangeable Word of God. When he saw them "limping" around the altar they had built, he mocked them, saying, perhaps your god is asleep, or on a journey, or maybe he has gone to the bathroom! God permitted such mockery not only because they were acting as fools but also because they were leading His people astray.

Elijah built his altar with twelve stones, remembering the acts of the Lord in delivering the twelve tribes of Israel. He then poured water on the burnt offering, repeating it three times. Then he offered his prayer to the Lord. His prayer was simple and powerful. He prayed that God would let it be known that He is both the Lord of history and the Lord of the present day. He asked God to confirm him as His servant who lived by the Word of the Lord and was sent by Him. Then he prayed that God would send fire so that all the people would know that the Lord alone is the true God.

The fire of God and the rain of God

"Then the fire of the Lord fell!" The fire brought life to the people of God. They fell on their faces and said, *"The Lord, He is God; the Lord, He is God!"* The fire brought life to God's people but death to His enemies.

We need the fire of the Holy Spirit to quicken our hearts, to restore our passion for God, and to empower us to be faithful to our calling. Mark, in his Gospel, reminds us of our calling. Jesus calls us for three reasons: to be with Him, to go out and preach, and to have authority to cast out demons. (Mark 3:13-15) Spiritual warfare is inherent in our calling. When does the fire of God come? When we commit everything to God in confidence and trust with full faith that He will give His Holy Spirit if we but ask! Then the fire of God will come to His Church once again.

The rain also began to fall. People needed the fire of God to restore their souls, but they also needed the rain to restore their crops and refresh their land. The rain comes with the fire! We need the great experience of welcoming the supernatural power of God into our lives by being baptized with His Holy Spirit. But we also need the constant, daily blessings that come from abiding in the Lord. This is the rain of God.

The prophet Joel tells us that the rain and the fire come together. (Joel 2:21-29) God gives the early rain for our vindication and the latter rain for our fruitfulness. The rains of God make up for us the "years that the swarming locust has eaten," what we might call our "lost years." The rains of God take away our shame. The fire of God enables us to experience the power of the Holy Spirit to become His effective witnesses to the world.

Watching in prayer

An aspect of spiritual warfare often overlooked by zealous people who seek only action and dynamic experiences when they engage in spiritual warfare is Elijah's time of "watching in prayer." Elijah watched in prayer before his battle with Jezebel's evil forces, and he watched in prayer as he continued to seek God for the rain He had promised to give. God used Elijah because he had learned to pray. (James 5:17-18) His prayer ministry is available to all Christians today.

Questions for Further Thought and Discussion
Please read 1 Kings 18:17-46
before answering these questions.

1. King Ahab saw Elijah as the "troubler of Israel." But Elijah replied that Ahab himself was the one troubling Israel because he had abandoned God's ways and followed the idol Baal. Yet Elijah was also troubling the nation of Israel by "turning their world upside down," just as Paul and Silas did in Thessalonica. (Acts 17:6) In what positive ways did Elijah, Paul and Silas turn their worlds upside down? Are Christians today turning the ungodly world upside down? If so, how is it happening? Do you see yourself as this kind of world changer?

2. In what ways did the Jews of Elijah's day compromise their faith by being "inclusive" of another religion? Are we as Christians called to be inclusive in our faith? If so, in what ways? If not, why not? What is the danger of relativism in contemporary Christianity?

3. As Christians we are called to be members of the "Community of the Holy Fire." The fire of God is the fire of His love. How does God use fire to reveal His love to His people? Have you experienced His purifying fire? How does God use fire to cause us to grow? How do you see the "fire of God" and the "rain of God" operating in your life?

Notes

Our Warfare

If we walk in the Lord, we will soon discover that we are engaged in spiritual warfare. We are promised that we will be attacked by Satan. (1 Peter 5:8-10) We are promised that we will suffer. But we also are promised that the rewards of our warfare will be great!

In war, we must be both defensive and offensive. (Read Ephesians 6:10-20.) The purpose is to remain standing. Many fall, but Christians do not stay down. We rise up again and continue to fight against the enemy. The object is not physical survival but spiritual survival. It is possible to survive spiritually even if the body dies. We win the battle by not losing the faith.

So we put on the "whole armor of God." It is not necessary to put on the armor each morning, like we would put on clothes, although some people go through the motions of putting on the armor symbolically or physically. But we already have the armor when we wake up each morning. Our armor is the things we *already have in Christ.* We must know our armor, both the defensive pieces and the offensive pieces:

Belt of Truth—This is the whole Word of God—God's truth, not our own. We overcome Satan by abiding in the Word. To do this we must *know* the Word, *trust* the Word and *use* the Word of God. Satan and his forces cannot stand against the truth that is revealed in the Word of God.

Breastplate of Righteousness—We have been made right with God by faith through the sacrifice of Jesus Christ. This righteousness comes from nothing within us. Christ Himself is our righteousness. (Romans 5:1)

Shoes for your feet—Shoes are for preaching the Gospel of peace. The first thing we should do if we are in Christian ministry is to buy a good pair of shoes. Romans 10:13-15 is the best explanation of the beauty of the feet of those who proclaim salvation.

Shield of Faith—Roman soldiers carried a small shield, but also a large shield the size of a door, one that could stop flaming arrows. By faith—obeying God and trusting Him to care for us—we can block the attacks of the enemy. We do not need *more* faith; we simply need to place our faith in Christ, the Rock of our salvation.

Helmet of Salvation—Paul is speaking here of God's salvation, which covers our minds, our bodies and our spirits and protects us against Satan's attacks.

Sword of the Spirit—This is the Word of God as the offensive weapon of our warfare. Notice that the whole armor of God begins and ends with the Word of God. The Belt of Truth is the Word of God in which we abide; the Sword of the Spirit is the *rhema* Word that the Spirit quickens to us in a particular situation. We go into the enemy's territory and proclaim the Word of God, as the *sword* of the Holy Spirit. Only the Spirit can make God's Word effective. The primary way to take territory from the enemy is to proclaim the Gospel in the power of the Holy Spirit, in the enemy's territory.

Praying at all times in the Spirit—Another piece of armor, not usually included, is prayer. Prayer is a weapon. While the Word of God is the *sword* of the Spirit, prayer is the *nuclear missile* of the Spirit. A sword will be effective at short range; a missile reaches the other side of the world. We are not speaking of the power of prayer, but rather of the power of *God* who hears and answers prayer!

To be victorious in warfare against Satan and his powers, we must cultivate the Word of God in our lives. Some ways to do that are:

- Receive the Word that the Holy Spirit implants in us, especially when we meditate on God's Word. (James 1:21)
- Rejoice in the Word of God, take delight in reading, studying and meditating on the Word. (Psalm 1:2; Psalm 19:10)
- Believe the Word of God and live by it, making it our standard in all matters.
- Obey the Word of God and be blessed in all we do. (James 1:22-25)
- Share the Word of God with others. Bless others with God's truth. (Ezra 7:10; Hebrews 5:12)

Chapter Six

Defeat in the Midst of Victory
1 Kings 19:1-4

*E*lijah enjoyed a major victory at Mount Carmel. At the end of the day, King Ahab was terrified, the people were turning to the Lord, and the major priests and prophets of Baal had been eliminated. This victory brought the beginning of reform, not just revival, to the nation.

Jezebel's death threat

But Elijah had a problem. It was not King Ahab, nor was it the prophets of Baal. The problem was a stronger power behind the throne: Jezebel. After telling Ahab to prepare his chariot and go down to Jezreel, Elijah then gathered up his garments and *ran* the seventeen miles down the mountain to Jezreel, arriving ahead of Ahab! Elijah may have been the first man to run the marathon! But we must wonder why he was in such a hurry to arrive in Jezreel, where Jezebel lived, ahead of Ahab. This may remain one of the unanswered questions in the Bible.

Soon after this victory, Jezebel delivered a death threat to Elijah. She had lost her religious and moral influence, and later she would become completely powerless. We will see later in our study that more people will have to be involved before the complete cleansing and reform would take place in Israel. But she had become entrenched and so was able to deliver the death threat. Elijah was afraid and ran for his life. (1 Kings 19:1-3) Fear, not doubt, is the greatest enemy of faith. Doubts may confuse us and weaken our effectiveness, but fear causes us to go backward into destruction. Faith alone is what enables us to always go forward, never going backward nor standing still, but always going forward toward the prize of the upward calling of God in Christ Jesus. (Hebrews 10:39)

We can learn a valuable lesson through Elijah's failure. Dr. Wallace once said in a lecture about Elijah that we could learn that "no one can fight God's battles without at times being involved in humiliating defeat in the midst of what seems to be great victory!"[6] We cannot enjoy victory and then immediately take a rest. The reason is that the enemy recovers quickly. A missionary working in a difficult-access nation added later that we can never take a "spiritual vacation," because great falls often come after great victories.

The cause of Elijah's fear

At the height of his power, Elijah collapsed. What was behind his failure? What was the cause of his fear? Ultimately, Satan is behind all Christian failures and fear. He is the enemy of our souls. Satan was defeated on the cross and his power was broken, but he still has power to persecute God's people. He knows that his time is short, so he continues to spread great wrath on the earth. (Revelation 12:7-12) Elijah was in the midst of great spiritual warfare, only this time it was for himself and not his nation. But against whom was Elijah fighting? Not against Jezebel, not against flesh and blood, but against Satan himself! The goal of spiritual warfare is described in Ephesians 6:13: *"Therefore, take up the whole armor of God, that you may be able to withstand in the evil day, and having done all, to stand firm."*

Elijah's flight exposed his fear. He went far south to Beersheba but still did not feel safe. Then he took a day's journey into the wilderness and sat down under a broom tree and prayed.

Notice how he prayed: *". . . I am no better than my fathers."* (1 Kings 19:4) He thought of Abraham and then remembered how Moses, after receiving the great revelation of God's law, discovered the gold calf and became so angry that he smashed the two tablets of the commandments; and again, he became so angry that he struck the rock to make water come out of it, rather than speaking to it, as God had commanded. He failed badly, and God was angry with him. Elijah considered how David had been chosen by God in a miraculous way and had won many victories, yet became so afraid of King Saul that he said, *"Fear and trembling come upon me, and horror overwhelms me. And I say, 'Oh, that I had wings like a dove! I would fly away and be at rest.'"* (Psalm 55:5-8)

What man or woman of God has not had such feelings, even after having been used greatly by God? Elijah knew all about Moses and David, both their mistakes and their sins. He knew all the principles. *But he never thought it could happen to him!* This may be a good word for young leaders today who think they are bringing in a "new era" of Christian ministry or mission to the world. We must learn from the past. Martin Buber, a Jewish philosopher-theologian, said: "History, as the world writes it, glorifies success, but the Bible glorifies those who have failed. The

Bible knows nothing of the intrinsic value of [worldly] success. On the contrary, when the Bible announces a successful deed, it always announces with the utmost detail, the failure involved in success."[7]

The greatest sin

Pride is the greatest of all sins, and there is no pride greater than *spiritual pride.* We may think that we have learned from our ancestors' mistakes and will now do better. We may feel that we have become much more whole, integrated people than some of the people we read about in the Bible or know about in history. But in reality we are all just broken, sick people who are continually being healed by the grace of God. Henri Nouwen summed it up when he said we all are "wounded healers."

The lesson of the cross

Elijah needed to be freed from arrogance and pride, from self-righteousness and from a judgmental spirit. He may not have been aware of these sins during his mighty battle on Mount Carmel, but now God was prepared to teach him the lessons of the cross. Now Elijah would be able to understand and identify with the disciples of Jesus. Even Jesus' disciples were not whole people. They were sick, in need of the Divine Physician. When Jesus informed them, at the Last Supper, that there was a traitor in their midst, the disciples were alarmed. Each saw something in himself that was weak, even to the point of betrayal of their Lord. Johann Sebastian Bach, in his St. Matthew's Passion, captured their fears when he composed a chorus in which each of the disciples cries out, "Is it I, Lord?" We ask again today, "Is it I, Lord?"

How did Jesus win the battle with Satan? He did not do it by obliterating the devil, which He easily could have done. Paul tells us, *"For indeed He was crucified because of weakness, yet He lives because of the power of God. For we also are weak in Him, yet we will live with Him because of the power of God directed toward you."* (2 Corinthians 13:4) Jesus was continuing the same battle Elijah had fought. This was why He was willing to suffer humiliation *even in victory!* Jesus defeated Satan totally, but He did so by sacrificing His life on the cross of Calvary.

The battle goes on. We have to fight today. If we take our eyes off Jesus who is the victor, we will fall just as Peter took his eyes off Jesus and fell after walking on the water at Jesus' command. But remember, your labor is not in vain. Nothing is really a failure for God, even in humiliation. So we should not be surprised when we suffer for the cause of the Gospel. Remember also that it is our weakness God wants, not our power. His power is made perfect in our weakness. (2 Corinthians 12:9-10)

We only need to have one great desire, but it must be a desire greater than all lesser desires. The Apostle Paul's desire was *"that I may know Him and the power of His resurrection, and may share His sufferings, becoming like Him in His death."* (Philippians 3:10) God responds to our desire by promising us that we can know Him. *"And we know that the Son of God has come and has given us understanding, so that we may know Him who is true; and we are in Him who is true, in His Son Jesus Christ."* (1 John 5:20) The more we know Him, the more we realize that we are only vessels of clay, easily broken. But our brokenness is a gift from God. Through it the treasure within us—Christ Himself—becomes visible to the world; people can see "that the surpassing power belongs to God and not to us." (2 Corinthians 4:7) The fruit of our brokenness is not only that God will use us more effectively to advance His

Kingdom throughout the world, but also that He will use our brokenness to lead us into healing and wholeness, so that we will be able to stand before His throne "without spot or wrinkle or any such thing, that [we] might be holy and without blemish" in His presence. (Ephesians 5:27)

Questions for Further Thought and Discussion
Please read 1 Kings 19:1-4
before answering these questions.

1. Why do you think Elijah was in such a hurry to go down to the city where Jezebel lived? What caused his great fear of Jezebel? Was his fear grounded in actual reality? Have you ever experienced such fear in your life or ministry?

2. Would you agree with Dr. Wallace's statement: "No one can fight God's battles without at times being involved in humiliating defeat in the midst of what seems to be great victory"? Have you found this to be true in your life? If so, what are some of the things you have learned?

3. What does it mean to you that Jesus was crucified "because of weakness"? (2 Corinthians 13:4) Why does God want our weakness rather than our strength? Can you think of an example in your own life when God used your brokenness to advance the cause of the Gospel?

Notes

Power in Ministry

Christian ministry is ministering in the power of the Holy Spirit. Luke 6:19 records that Jesus ministered in power: *"And all the crowd sought to touch Him, for power came out from Him and healed them all."* His power came from His intimacy with His Father, through dwelling in His presence. Jesus' greatest joy was fellowship with His Father, and He often would separate Himself from the crowds after ministering to them to go out and be alone with His Father. Often He spent the night in prayer. Not only was this the source of power for Jesus, but it is also the only source of power for every Christian.

Yet Paul tells us that Jesus was "crucified in weakness." (2 Corinthians 13:4) Jesus had all power to crush the devil and His enemies, but He did not use that power to defend Himself. Instead, He submitted Himself fully to His Father's will, which was that He was to lay down His life as a ransom for the sins of mankind. He did not count equality with God a thing to be grasped, but made Himself nothing, taking the form of a servant. (Philippians 2:6-7)

In the passage we are studying today, God is allowing Elijah to suffer, to be afraid, and to lose confidence in himself, to enable him to see that the remarkable power that marked Elijah's ministry was from God and not from himself. God was honored later by the Apostle Paul when he confessed, *"For when I am weak, then I am strong."* (2 Corinthians 12:10)

Chapter Seven

Victory in the Midst of Defeat
1 Kings 19:5-18

⟨❀⟩

*G*od remains the God of victory even in the midst of the failure of man. Elijah's fall seemed to be a setback. Elijah was lonely and depressed to the point of wanting to die. But God remained in control. He continued to work His purpose out in Elijah's day just as He does today. His great purpose is to create a people with whom He can dwell.

> *God is working His purpose out*
> *as year succeeds to year;*
> *God is working his purpose out,*
> *and the time is drawing near;*
> *Nearer and nearer draws the time,*
> *the time that shall surely be,*
> *When the earth shall be filled with the glory of God*
> *As the waters cover the sea.*
>
> Words by Arthur C. Ainger
> Music by Martin F. Shaw

True victory and true success

God healed Elijah in the midst of his defeat. He was leading him to true success. But what is true biblical success? What is the biblical concept of prosperity? Psalm 1 teaches us that the one who meditates on the Word of God will prosper in all that he does. But the psalmist is not promising a long life free from illness, or a problem-free life of financial luxury. On the contrary, the Bible does promise us that we will be blessed by suffering. *"For it has been granted to you that for the sake of Christ you should not only believe in Him but also suffer for His sake."* (Philippians 1:29)

Success must always be measured by the degree to which God's will prospers in our life. Jesus Christ, the Suffering Servant, was the truly successful man. Isaiah the prophet spoke of Jesus in this way: *"the will of the Lord shall prosper in his hand."* (Isaiah 53:10) This is the true biblical definition of success. The will of the Lord prospered in Elijah's hand when he defeated the false prophets on Mount Carmel. God's will prospered, so Elijah prospered and was successful even though he collapsed and was ready to give up. Now God was ready to restore Elijah, and Elijah would see that even in the midst of his great failure, God's will prospered and would continue to do so.

God's plans for Elijah's ministry

Jezebel's death threat triggered Elijah's collapse. She felt secure again, and she was angry. She was determined, as a daughter of Satan, to destroy Elijah. But God was determined to restore him to fullness of life and ministry.

During this time of Elijah's crisis, God may have spoken the same words to Elijah that His Son, Jesus, later spoke to Simon Peter. *"Simon, Simon, behold, Satan demanded to have you, that he might sift you like wheat, but I have prayed for you that your faith may not fail. And when you have turned again, strengthen your brothers."* (Luke 22:31-32) Satan planned to destroy Elijah. But Jesus prayed! And God restored Simon Peter, just as He restored Elijah.

However, Peter's and Elijah's responses before they were restored were opposite. Peter was overly self-confident (Luke 22:33), and Elijah was despondent. The writer of Hebrews shows the proper response to God's discipline. *"My son, do not regard lightly the discipline of the Lord [Peter], nor be weary when reproved by Him [Elijah]. For the Lord disciplines the one He loves, and chastises every son whom He receives. . . . He disciplines us for our good, that we may share His holiness."* (Hebrews 12:4-10)

God turned Jezebel's death threat around and used it to heal Elijah rather than to allow him to be destroyed! He used it to prepare him for the next stage in his ministry. Elijah had forgotten God's promises, but God had not. *"No weapon that is fashioned against you shall succeed."* (Isaiah 54:17) Satan works at times directly, and at other times through ungodly people to fashion weapons—threats, curses or other tools—to destroy God's people. God, however, destroys the plans of the enemy that are designed to destroy His people. Joseph was able to forgive his brothers who had betrayed him and sold him into slavery, because he knew that God had turned their evil plans into good. The Jewish scholar Everett Fox, in his translation *The Five Books of Moses*, says, *"Now you, you planned ill against me, but God planned-it-over for good, in order to do (as is) this very day—to keep many people alive!"* (Genesis 50:20) God lays *His* plans over the plans of men, destroying the enemy's plans. God lays *His blessing* over the *curses and attacks* of Satan. Today also, we can intercede boldly and with confidence for those who have had a curse placed upon them by ungodly people, or who have been threatened with death or other attacks. God, who works all things together for good for those who love Him and who are called according to His purposes, will bless His weak and vulnerable people in innumerable ways. (Romans 8:28)

Elijah's loneliness and depression were caused by his self-pity and self-righteousness. His pride led him into self-pity and made him believe that he was indispensable, and that he was the source of power. Self-righteousness is actually "hardened self-pity." *"I have been very zealous for the Lord. . . and I alone am left."* (1 Kings 19:10)

God was very firm but very gentle with Elijah as He began to restore him. He dealt with him tenderly and with great patience. We find no trace of judgment or condemnation from God, but rather a great outpouring of His love on Elijah. God began to restore Elijah in his mind and spirit so that He could give him a clear understanding of what had happened to him and to his people. He brought Elijah back in touch with His healing power as He gently led him to see the great power of the Holy Spirit still working within him. God was not finished with Elijah!

God's seven-step method of restoration

Let us examine God's pattern of therapy for "burned-out Elijah." He used a seven-fold method of restoration for His servant.

Step 1: God caused Elijah to sleep. (1 Kings 19:5) *"It is in vain that you rise up early and go late to rest, eating the bread of anxious toil; for He gives to His beloved sleep."*

(Psalm 127:2) Sleep can sometimes be an escape, and we must be aware of the danger. But greater than the danger of sleep are the many benefits of sleep. Sleep is essential for both physical and emotional healing. God was in total control of Elijah as he slept, and He was able to minister directly to his spirit.

Step 2: God ministered to Elijah through an angel. (I Kings 19:5-8) *"Are [angels] not all ministering spirits, sent out to serve for the sake of those who will inherit salvation?"* (Hebrews 1:14) Elijah awoke as he felt the angel touch him. The angel fed him and gave him water to drink. We can imagine Jesus appearing to His disciples after the resurrection, by the shores of the Sea of Galilee. He ministered to His disciples in much the same way His Father's angels had ministered to Elijah many centuries before. He had breakfast ready for His discouraged and frustrated disciples and revealed His love to them. Elijah ate and slept again. The angel woke Elijah a second time, to feed him miraculous food. Perhaps this was the first "health food." This food would enable him to travel for forty days and nights! We must expect angels to minister to us when we serve the Lord, and also when we are exhausted and discouraged. We may *expect to meet* angels at some time in our earthly journey. The first two steps of God's therapy involved simply meeting Elijah's physical needs.

Step 3: God sent Elijah on a long journey to Mount Horeb. (1 Kings 19:8) The journey took nearly three months to complete, so God was deliberately forcing Elijah to take some time off from his intense work and busy life. During this time he was out of touch with the political and religious problems of his nation; he was separated from his "missionary work."

Elijah knew that God was sending him to Mount Horeb because that was where Moses had received his call. He was going back into history to see the miraculous ways God had led His people out of Egypt and through the wilderness. Mountains are often the places where God gives revelation in the Scriptures, and they remain today places where pilgrims can draw near to God. God led him to a cave. It could have been the cave where God had given Moses the vision of His glory, when He hid him in the cleft of the rock.

Elijah would soon discover that his work did not suffer at all while he was gone! This is because it was *God's work*, not Elijah's. God is so much in control of all affairs that He can give His people the holidays they need. Would it not bring renewal to the Church today if not only pastors and missionaries but also all Christians could trust God enough to take time off when they are tired and weary? Surely we all can find some time during a day to take time to "rest in God," or to take a day off as a family to bring healing and wholeness into the home. God would bless our families greatly if we would take a few weeks, or even a few days, off during the year to allow Him to restore and re-energize us. God's therapy for Elijah extends to His people today.

Step 4: God asked Elijah a question. (1 Kings 19:9) God led him to a cave, where the Word of the Lord came to him. *"What are you doing here, Elijah?"* God was trying to get Elijah to understand where he was coming from, and to give him a greater understanding of what had happened to him and what God planned to do. God was asking Elijah to share with Him what was in his heart and mind.

In seeking healing, it is important not only to ask, "Why, Lord?" but to allow God to ask the questions of us.

Healing may come more readily by listening to the Lord than by simply pouring out our heart to Him. God's questions themselves can be healing. But Elijah answered with the same self-pity and complaining attitude as before. God was unable to get any change out of Elijah with His question. God would ask the same question again, later, but in a different way.

Step 5: God spoke to Elijah in a low murmuring sound that was like the sound of a gentle stillness. (1 Kings 19:11-13) We can sense a change beginning to come over Elijah. On Mount Carmel he had been bold and daring and seemed to move on his own initiative. Now he was more passive and submissive, following wherever God led him. God was dealing very gently with him and leading him into a new phase of ministry. We can sense this because of the way God spoke. He did not speak in the earthquake, wind or fire—the patterns to which Elijah had been accustomed. God was teaching Elijah that He could work in ways that were not spectacular and earth-shaking yet were equally powerful to change the hearts of men and advance His Kingdom on earth.

Elijah had been accustomed to the mighty signs of God in earthquakes and fire and had identified the presence of God in those things. Now Elijah stood in awe and wonder at the stillness of the silence that overcame him. He discovered in that silence the presence of the Lord, without any accompanying signs. God was present *in His Word!*

The Church today needs to recover the power of silence. Biblical silence is not merely the absence of words, the lack of noise or just wondering what to say next. The silence of God is the silence of the heart. God is calling us today to take time daily to lay aside our worries and concerns, to turn from our sins and remove the noisy obstacles in our hearts, and turn our ears to listen to all that He wants to say to us. This is the silence He seeks: to kneel before His Word and listen, as Elijah did.

Silence can be compared to space in Asian art. Space in Asian art is not empty, nor is it incomplete. On the contrary, space is as important as the drawing surrounding it. In the spiritual world, this space is called "silence." Silence is the home of the Word. Where there is no silence, there is no Word.

God spoke to Elijah in the silence. He first asked Elijah the same question He had previously asked him, "What are you doing here, Elijah?" But a change had begun to come over Elijah. His anger and self-righteous attitude were gone. He began to listen. In his silence he heard the Lord calling to him in love. Ronald S. Wallace said it this way: "God's presence with us today, which is often realized through a quietly spoken word—the still small voice! —is the only token we need that He loves and forgives us, wants to cure us of our depression and that our labor is not in vain."[8]

The great manifestations of Mount Carmel were no longer to be the mark of Elijah's ministry. Rather, he was to enter into a more mundane, everyday life of submissive ministry. But Elijah knew that the God who had answered his prayers in such a spectacular manner before the prophets of Baal, and the God who answered his prayers for famine, for rain and fire, would continue to answer his prayers as he walked daily with His Lord.

Elijah did not turn his back on the spectacular miracles God had worked through him. God would perform another mighty miracle at the end of his life by taking him up into heaven in a whirlwind. Now, however, Elijah was prepared to obey all the commands of God even when they seemed ordinary. He was ready to allow God to decide the form his ministry should take.

Christians today remain divided in the way they seek to serve God. Some must see great signs and wonders to be convinced that God is really present. Others long for personal growth and a quiet life without God's signs and wonders. But Elijah did not make the mistake of attempting to dictate how God should manifest His presence with him. Neither did the believers in the Early Church. The Holy Spirit came with a mighty wind, and with signs and wonders; He continues to do the same today. The Pentecostal churches are the fastest-growing churches in the world today. We need the Pentecostal experience of the baptism with the Holy Spirit; but along with it, we always must go back to the Word of God, where God speaks to us daily in quiet meditation, to fully enter the presence of God and stand in awe before His majesty, His holiness and His love.

Step 6: God gave Elijah a new task. (1 Kings 19:15-17) His new task would not be as sensational and visible as before, but it would be equally important. Much remained to be done in order to complete the reformation God desired, and it would still require battles and the shedding of blood. But Elijah would no longer be involved in these battles. His new job may have seemed "ordinary" to him, but it was equally important. His most important task now was to "strengthen his brothers." (Luke 22:31-32)

First, he was to anoint Hazael king over Syria and Jehu as future king of Israel. Then he was to anoint Elisha as his successor. There were many other young prophets among Elijah's "School of the Prophets," but he was not to choose his successor. God had already called His man. Elijah simply was to listen and obey. God had a long-term plan for each of these three men. Each would play a significant role that would bring ruin to King Ahab and Queen

Jezebel and eradicate the prophets of Baal from the land of Israel. God was now expanding the way He worked. Until now He had used only Elijah, but now He was using a team. Actually, Elijah did not anoint Hazael and Jehu; God took him up in the whirlwind first. He anointed only Elisha; then Elisha anointed the other two.

The significance of this step in Elijah's healing was the fact that God still had work that He wanted Elijah to do. He was not finished with him because of his mistakes, just as He is not finished with His people today who make mistakes and commit sins, provided that they turn back to Him with contrite hearts.

Elijah is now on his way to full recovery. Having work to do is part of the therapy of restoration. Elijah did not just "sit around and wait until he was fully restored."[9] He listened eagerly to God and obeyed all that God told him to do.

Step 7: God led Elijah into community! (1 Kings 19:18) God told Elijah that He had a "Hidden Church" of seven thousand members who had not bowed to Baal! One of the key elements in healing and restoration is having fellowship with other believers. Elijah's problem was that he had been a loner. But he discovered that there is a limit to how much loneliness a person can endure, regardless of how strong or faithful that person may be. God told him that he no longer had to bear the burden alone.

Henri Nouwen remarked that the Christian life means to die.[9] He pointed out that the fear of dying at the end of our lives might not be so fearful if we can die well now! He says, "The real death—the passing from time into eternity—has to be made now."[9] God has sent people to be close to us to help us gradually let go of the world, and of the sins that seek to overwhelm us, so that we may be truly free to serve God. We cannot be missionaries alone, whether we are in a foreign land or whether we are serving God in our own homeland. We must become a community of love.

This seven-step healing program of God is available to all His disciples today. It is God's proven plan for restoration: Take rest, with needed sleep for mind and body. Be open to angelic ministry. Take time away from work and responsibilities to enjoy the presence of God and to have time with family and friends. Listen to God as He speaks in silence. Abide in His Word. Obey everything God says to do with joy. Be open to the new tasks God may want to give you. And enjoy the fellowship of believers.

Questions for Further Thought and Discussion
Please read 1 Kings 19:5-18
before answering these questions.

1. Do you agree that the biblical understanding of the successful person is one in whose hand the will of the Lord prospers? Can we be truly successful even when the visible results of our ministry seem to be a failure? Do you consider yourself successful? If so, in what way?

2. What are some instances in your life when Satan has planned evil against you but God has laid His good and perfect plans on top of Satan's plans, to work everything for good? Share with another person or group how God transformed an evil situation into a time of blessings.

3. Think back over God's seven-step plan of healing and restoration for Elijah. Which steps are helpful to you in your own life? Explain the reasons you think they are helpful. Do you feel that you have the necessary "space" in your lifestyle that enables you to walk in intimacy with the Lord?

Notes

Angels

Both the Old and New Testaments abound in references to angelic activity, both as worshipers of God and as ministers to God's people. The highest calling of angels is to worship God. God the Father commanded all of His angels to worship God the Son, Jesus. *"Let all God's angels worship Him."* (Hebrews 1:6) The Apostle John recounts his vision of the Conquering Lamb, Jesus Christ, in the following way: *"Then I looked, and I heard around the throne. . . the voice of many angels, numbering myriads of myriads and thousands of thousands, saying with a loud voice, 'Worthy is the Lamb who was slain, to receive power and wealth and wisdom and might and honor and glory and blessing!'"* (Revelation 5:11-12) Likewise, when an angel of the Lord appeared to the shepherds at Jesus' birth and announced the Good News, there suddenly appeared with the angel *"a multitude of the heavenly host praising God and saying, 'Glory to God in the highest, and on earth peace among those with whom He is pleased!'"* (Luke 2:8-14)

Angels are not only worshipers; they also are messengers to deliver God's Word to His people. *"He makes His messengers winds, His ministers a flaming fire."* (Psalm 104:4) The angel Gabriel announced to young Mary that she was to become the mother of our Lord. Then an angel appeared to Joseph assuring him that it was the Holy Spirit who had conceived the child in Mary's womb. (Matthew 1:19-25) The psalmist tells us that angels are mighty ones who *do God's Word,* who *obey the voice of His Word* and *do His will.* (Psalm 103:20-21).

Angels also guide, guard and protect, and minister to the needs of God's people. *"For He will command His angels concerning you to guard you in all your ways."*

(Psalm 91:11) An angel appeared to Jesus in the Garden of Gethsemane and strengthened Him. (Luke 22:43) Likewise, an angel fed Elijah when he was at the lowest point of his life in the wilderness. Children have guardian angels to protect and guide them. (Matthew 18:10) Even adults have angels who care for them, as evidenced by the reaction of the Early Christian community when Peter was released from prison, as they tried to correct the servant girl Rhoda by saying, *"You are out of your mind. . . . It is [Peter's] angel."* (Acts 12:15)

With such clear and abundant evidence, we should be open to the ministry of angels today, at a time when Satan's angels are so strongly attacking the Church of the Living God.

Chapter Eight

The Call of God
1 Kings 19:19-21

❧✦❧

*E*very Christian has a call of God on his or her life. We are called to belong to His Son, Jesus Christ. We are called to be holy and to belong to His family, the "community of the Holy Fire." God also calls each of us for unique tasks that will advance His Kingdom in the world. Jesus made it very clear to His disciples that they were not the ones who chose Him, but rather He chose and called them. *"You did not choose Me, but I chose you and appointed you that you should go and bear fruit and that your fruit should abide, so that whatever you ask the Father in My name, He may give it to you."* (John 15:16)

God of both the valleys and the mountains

God had already healed and restored Elijah from his severe loneliness and depression. Through that time of healing Elijah learned many lessons, not least of which was that God is with us both on the mountaintops and in the valleys. The Syrian army was soon to learn this lesson literally, when they later assembled in a mountainous region to wage war against Israel. A prophet of the Lord told King Ahab to go out and fight, and that Israel would be victorious. After Syria suffered defeat, the servants of Syria's king told him that they had lost because Israel's God was a "God of the mountains but not of the valleys." So Syria once again attacked Israel in the valleys, only to suffer an even greater defeat than before. (1 Kings 20:13-30) King David may have remembered this promise of the Lord when he wrote, *"Even though I walk through the valley of the shadow of death, I will fear no evil, for You are with me."* (Psalm 23:4)

The call of Elisha

Elijah was ready to begin the new work that God had given him to do. Not far away, in the village of Abel-Meholah, a man named Shaphat was living with his son, Elisha; they both hated Baal worship as much as Elijah. Elisha probably had been present at Mount Carmel when the great battle took place. Elisha and the servants were plowing with twelve yoke of oxen; Elisha's was the twelfth plough, the place of the son of the owner of an important estate. They were probably talking about the great victory at Mount Carmel and rejoicing over the rain that had brought an end to the famine.

Suddenly Elijah appeared. He paused in front of Elisha and threw his cloak over him. No words needed to be spoken. Elisha and all the others knew what this meant: He had been chosen to become Elijah's successor, and He must leave everything, follow Elijah and submit to his training. He had a costly decision to make, and he made it immediately. He only wanted to bid farewell to his mother and father.

In the New Testament, Jesus' call to Peter, James and John, as well as Matthew, sounds almost like an echo of

Elijah's call to Elisha. In the Gospel of John, John never pays much attention to the time of day things happen. But when he and his brother James had their first conversation with Jesus, he considered it so important that he recorded the time of day! (John 1:39)

Inner call and outer call

Was Elisha expecting Elijah? Was he aware of a call of God on his life? The answer would have to be yes, because God had already called Elisha. Elisha knew deep within his spirit when Elijah called him that this was God! God had prepared Elisha for Elijah's *outer call* by giving him an *inner call,* a deep conviction of personal calling from God. This was why he "left his oxen and ran after Elijah." Every Christian needs an inner calling direct from God in order to respond to an outer calling from another person. In later years, in times of doubts and crises that shake our faith, we cannot fall back on an *outer call* alone. The fact that we may have been called by a church or a denomination, or by a mission organization, will not give much assurance in such times if we have not also been called by *God!* We must be able to fall back on the clear knowledge that Jesus Himself has personally called us. He alone is our certainty. Then we can go forward with boldness and determination.

God is the one who told Elijah to call Elisha. Elijah simply obeyed by casting his mantle over Elisha. Elijah's call was to announce to Elisha that God had called him and that he must obey. The decision was costly for Elisha. He had to give up family and home, a settled life with wealth. He had the possibility of saying no to God, but he responded with readiness.

Go back home

But Elijah did not allow Elisha to follow him. Instead he said, *"Go back again, for what have I done to you?"* This could be translated to read, "Go back home, but remember what I have done to you." Elijah was a man with a strong personality and had always worked alone. It would have been easy for him to dominate Elisha and even intimidate him into leaving everything to follow him immediately. When a leader with a strong, sometimes overpowering personality controls a younger follower by requiring him to obey him completely, this makes the young disciple unable to make personal decisions at the feet of Jesus Christ. This results in a terrible injustice to God as well as to the young disciple's dignity.

Elijah did not dominate Elisha. He was a mature and devout man of God who made room for younger disciples to follow him. Paul, fully aware of Elijah's maturity in working with others, said, *"What then is Apollos? What is Paul? Servants through whom you believed, as the Lord assigned to each. I planted, Apollos watered, but God gave the growth. So neither he who plants nor he who waters is anything, but only God who gives the growth."* (1 Corinthians 3:5-7) We can learn from Elijah, the man of God, how to give advice to others without controlling them. This will free young leaders to become all that God intends them to be.

Elisha was free to choose God without any persuasion of man. But he knew that his life was no longer his own. He had to listen to God and obey what He said to do. He could never again speak only what he thought or do what he simply wanted to do. He was called to be the servant of the Lord who enjoyed the absolute love of God but who also stood under the absolute authority of God. This was not only the hour of the announcement of *God's decision about Elisha*; it was also the hour of *Elisha's decision about God.*

Elisha's preparation to leave

Elijah was wise to allow Elisha time to consider his call and make preparations to leave. As we respond to God's call today, we also need to remember the importance of maintaining our relations with family and other friends, letting them know what God is doing, what His calling is in our lives, and how He is working to bring it about. If Elisha had left without proper relationships or without taking time to bid his farewells, it would have been a day of sadness, anger, tensions and gloom. But because he left in the right way, it was a day of rejoicing and thanksgiving; everybody was able to be a part of the great things God was planning to do through His servant Elisha.

Elisha demonstrated how well he understood what had happened to him. He prepared a farewell banquet by slaying his oxen and using the yokes as the wood to make the fire to boil them in. He sacrificed his oxen, which had been most precious to him in providing his and his family's needs. He broke the yokes, signifying that he would not return again to his old way of life. He "burned the bridges" to his old life and was ready to begin anew.

It would be ten long years of apprenticeship before Elisha could begin his own ministry. He would work as an assistant to Elijah and seek to learn everything from him. He did not immediately go out and start his own ministry; rather, he served. He would learn what it means to be a servant leader. But we know that later on, young Elisha's ministry was even greater than that of the older Elijah's. The number of miracles was doubled! There was more power, perhaps more creativity in his ministry.

He worked in similar ways as Elijah, but he was not the same. God did a new thing in Elisha.

The mission 4/14 window

There are many young potential leaders waiting to be confirmed in their calling to serve God for the evangelization of the world, and the great majority of them are between the ages of four and fourteen years old! Luis Bush, one of the leading missiologists in the world today, was the creator of the 10/40 missions window, focused on the geographical location of unreached people groups. Now he has replaced the 10/40 window with the "4/14 window." He reported that one-third of today's world population is under fifteen years old. "It is time to wake up," he said. "We must reach, rescue and raise up this generation! Eighty percent of all people make a decision for Christ as children." He continued, "Now it is young people's time! The 4/14ers are on center stage throughout the world!"[10]

Two key elements in raising up children and youth are *decision* and *formation,* according to Luis Bush. One reason it is becoming more urgent to encourage children to make a decision for Jesus Christ is that a high percentage of fifteen-year-olds are planning to leave the Church, either permanently or for a long period of time. For this reason, we might call the 4/14 window a "golden window of opportunity." Formation of Christian character begins early, and children require mentors who will love them and instruct them in the truth that will set them free to become powerful servants of God.

We do not know how old Elisha was when Elijah first called him. He was probably a young man, since he was plowing in his father's field when he was called. The most important thing to remember is that Elijah nurtured and taught Elisha for ten years before releasing him into ministry. This enabled Elisha to form a biblical worldview that would later enable him to confront the forces of evil surrounding him with God's thoughts and not his own.

These two elements—*decision* and *formation*—are keys to prepare today's young leaders to rise up to God's calling to challenge the "Jezebels" of our age and to advance the Kingdom of God throughout the world. We can learn from Elijah how to call these young disciples into the service of the King.

Questions for Further Thought and Discussion
Please read 1 Kings 19:19-21
before answering these questions.

1. Describe God's call on your life. Are you aware of a specific time He called you to serve Him? Or did you have a gradual understanding of God's purposes for your life?

2. What does this story of Elisha's call have to say to a young person today who may be called by God to a "difficult-access" nation as a missionary, but whose family opposes her going? What does it say to the parents of such a person? What is the biblical position in such a situation?

3. We have said that *decision* and *formation* are two key ingredients for releasing young people into missions today. These two elements are essential for anyone, anywhere, who seeks to follow God's will and be fruitful for Him. Are you clear about your decision to follow Christ wherever He may lead you? What are you doing about forming a biblical worldview to enable you to minister in wisdom and power to the world?

Notes

Biblical Christian Formation

Gary Parrett and S. Steve Kang[11] speak of the need for *formation of the heart* when receiving truth. They exhort teachers to not merely transfer knowledge to the students but to go further and help students to begin unearthing false assumptions about biblical truth, and to help students "create space" through the power of silence and searching questions.

Their approach indicates that the Word of God is central to the development of a genuine Christian worldview. We must first of all listen to God's Word on a daily basis, then allow that Word to clear away the distortions of truth that lie deep within us. Then we must obey the Word faithfully and allow God's Word to *remold us into the image of Jesus Christ.* Jesus spoke to people's hearts, saying, *"Now that you know these things, you will be blessed if you do them."* (John 13:17, NIV) Obedience leads to greater blessing, both for ourselves and for the world.

We must act on what we study and meditate upon; our contemplation must lead us into action. This means that the Church must turn away from two things: One is the tendency to be activity-oriented without waiting in the presence of the Lord in order to do *His* will rather than our own. The other is the tendency to be satisfied with mere intellectual knowledge or "proper doctrinal understanding" that does not lead to obedient action. The need is urgent for the Church to create a new approach to ministry that leads people to be "brokenhearted before the Word" so that their hearts can be "warmed by the Word" in a way that causes them to delight in obeying what God says.

There are many other elements necessary for biblical formation. Reading good books that provide foundational Christian teaching, becoming a part of a Bible study group, developing responsible, caring and accountable community life, witnessing to our faith, performing acts of mercy and justice for the poor and other "voiceless people" of the world, and other spiritual disciplines.

Chapter Nine

A Double Portion of the Spirit
2 Kings 2:1-15

᪥

*T*he Scriptures speak of King Ahab as "a man who sold his soul." After listening to the prophets who told him to be bold in facing the attacks of the king of Syria, he obeyed and was victorious. But rather than turning wholly to the Lord, he began to court the friendship of that same king, who was a professed enemy of God. Then, when the wicked queen Jezebel murdered Naboth in order to take his vineyard illegally, he had the opportunity to repent. Instead he allowed himself to be drawn more deeply under the power of the wicked queen Jezebel than ever before. The writer of Second Kings adds a comment: *"There was none who sold himself to do what was evil in the sight of the Lord like Ahab, whom Jezebel his wife incited."* (1 Kings 21:25) King Ahab was the "man who *sold himself.*" Jesus later added, *"For what does it profit a man to gain the whole world and forfeit his soul?"* (Mark 8:36)

As Elijah's life drew to an end, the Scriptures remind us of the power of a depraved mind, like Jezebel, and of a compromising spirit, like Ahab who "sold his soul" to do the evil that was the will of his wife. Jezebel was a woman without a conscience, seemingly beyond the possibility of repentance. Do we not discover the same "spirit of Jezebel" in our world today? Do we not find that spirit in people who have depraved minds such as Jezebel had, who are determined to destroy justice, to cause God's people to turn toward satanic ways, to corrupt children and young people with the power of pornography and child sex trafficking, and who are determined to annihilate God's loving purposes throughout the whole world?

We can understand the degree of the depravity of both ancient and modern man only when we interpret it through the light of the New Testament, not the Old Testament. Jezebel could not have been that evil in her own power. She was totally controlled by the power of Satan, whom Jesus called "a murderer from the beginning." The Apostle Paul spoke of men and women who were under the bondage of Satan and who would wreak havoc in the world. "Watch and pray," says the Apostle Peter, *". . . your adversary the devil prowls around like a roaring lion, seeking someone to devour."* (1 Peter 5:8)

Timing for new leadership

The time had come for new leadership. Elijah's work was finished. He had only a few more hours on this earth before being taken up to heaven in a whirlwind. He had been a mighty leader for the nation in a time of deep crisis. But it would take different leadership to complete the reform of the nation. God had plans then, as He does today, to take the new generation of leaders into the next level of ministry, a step farther than the older generation. One of the things we have always taught missionaries working in cross-cultural nations is that the first thing they should do upon arrival in their new land is begin searching and praying for potential leaders, leaders who would be able to take the ministry to a new and higher level than the missionary himself could do. We urge them to not choose leaders because of their outward appearance or charismatic personalities, or their language ability, or their smoothness of operation; rather they are to search for young men and women who love God more than their own lives, who are pure in heart and who are willing to stake their lives on the Word of God, men and women of prayer, who have a heart of compassion for the poor and needy and a heart of passion for the extension of the Kingdom of God. Should this not be the criteria for choosing new leaders in every church throughout the world, and in every Christian ministry?

Elisha was the man. He had shown himself to be teachable and dependable. For ten long years he had been a faithful servant to Elijah, following in his shadow. Elijah knew he was ready. But Elisha was still an "untried man" in battle against the forces of evil. The question that lingered in Elijah's mind was, "Does Elisha have what it takes to be a leader of his people?"

Transfer of leadership

Two issues confront those who are involved in change of leadership, especially when it involves passing on leadership from one generation to the next. The first is *continuity* and the second is *letting go of authority*. The outgoing leader must relinquish his leadership and let go of his authority. But the new leader must not only acknowledge but also fully embrace the God-given vision of the ministry and continue the traditions on which it was founded. Each generation must acknowledge and be willing to learn from the other.

Elijah had always had his greatest moments in solitude. Now he wants to be alone with God. Three times he pleaded with Elisha to leave him alone and let him go on several journeys to hear from God. But three times Elisha refused to leave; he could not bear to be left alone. Elijah was the most important person in Elisha's life. Elisha had left his earthly father; now Elijah had become his spiritual father. He used Elijah's own expression in refusing: *"As the Lord lives, and as you yourself live, I will not leave you!"*

God knew that Elisha needed to learn the history of how He had led His people in the past. They had just visited Gilgal, where Joshua and his people had camped after crossing the Jordan River. There Joshua and his people had set up twelve stones as a memorial, to inform their children how the Lord dried up the waters of the Jordan, just as He had done at the Red Sea. This was where God commanded the fathers to circumcise all the males born in the wilderness, as a sign that God had "rolled away the reproach of Egypt"—all the guilt, condemnation and fear that had marked their lives. (Joshua 4:19-24) Elisha may have thought of how God had recently "rolled away the reproach of Baal."

The second place they visited was Bethel, where Abraham had built an altar after God had made a covenant with him. (Genesis 12:8) Later, Jacob had wrestled there with the angel of God in a life-changing encounter. Elisha began to understand that Bethel was the "house of God."

Finally they arrived at Jericho. (Joshua 5:13-6:27) This was where Joshua had won his first major victory in the Promised Land. There he met the "commander of the army of the Lord," who told him to take off his sandals because he was standing on holy ground.

Elijah took Elisha with him across the Jordan, which was his final destination. Elijah performed his last miracle there; he took off his cloak and struck the water. Immediately the water was parted and they crossed over on dry ground. The River Jordan remains today as the sign of the ultimate entry of God's people into glory. "Crossing the Jordan" is symbolic of passing from this life to a higher life. Elisha must have known that he himself was standing on holy ground. He knew that God was calling him to a higher destiny that must be completed before he would "cross the Jordan" into glory as Elijah was about to do.

Elisha felt weak and totally unprepared. He was keenly aware of his inadequacies, more than ever before. He knew that he had passion and zeal, and that he had learned much from his time with Elijah. But still he was not ready for what lay ahead. He knew there was something he needed if he was to face the future alone and become God's "threshing sledge, new [and] sharp," (Isaiah 41:15) to eradicate the power of evil from his nation and to bring needed reform.

Elisha was not alone in his anxiety. Every man, woman or child who knows God and who has been called to do great exploits for Him suffers the same sense of helpless anxiety. Jesus' disciples had lived with, served and ministered with the Lord Himself for three years. Yet they were not prepared when He was taken from them. Most Bible school or theological seminary students, after completing three or four years of intensive study of the Bible and the doctrines of the Church, are not ready for ministry when they graduate. Like many of us who have preceded them, they have much head knowledge but little heart knowledge of the things of God. Many Christians serve the Lord and their churches for twenty or thirty years but still remain unprepared to be used by God for the maximum of what He wants.

A double portion of the Spirit

"Ask what I shall do for you, before I am taken from you," said Elijah. Elisha did not hesitate but immediately answered, *"Please let there be a double portion of your spirit on me!"* He was asking that a "double portion" of the Holy Spirit who was in Elijah be upon him also. Elisha knew he had to receive the Holy Spirit in *abundant measure,* to the full extent to which he was entitled as a servant of God. He did not ask for more knowledge, or only to understand methods of ministry. He did not ask how to be an effective manager of many people. Elisha had seen that Elijah had succeeded not because he was courageous, and certainly not because he had organizational ability. Elijah was effective for one reason only: the Holy Spirit! Elisha understood what Zechariah meant when he told the people how to rebuild their nation: *"Not by might, nor by power, but by My Spirit, says the Lord of hosts."* (Zechariah 4:6)

Elisha had all he needed on the horizontal, or human, level. He needed the vertical gift, the gift that God alone could give. He needed the *full portion* of God's Spirit that Jesus promises to all who trust in Him. *"For John baptized with water, but you will be baptized with the Holy Spirit not many days from now. . . . You will receive power when the Holy Spirit has come upon you, and you will be My witnesses in Jerusalem and in all Judea and Samaria, and to the end of the earth."* (Acts 1:5, 8) Elijah's reply was, "You have asked a hard thing." This is because it is impossible for any human to transmit the Holy Spirit of God to another.

After Elisha asked for the empowering of the Holy Spirit who was in Elijah, and after receiving Elijah's answer, the Scriptures tell us that as *"they went on and talked, chariots of fire and horses of fire separated the two of them. And Elijah went up by a whirlwind into heaven."* They *went on and talked.* The "last walk" of mentor and disciple! This was the most precious moment for both of them in the transfer of leadership. Elijah undoubtedly opened his mind to Elisha in a way he had never done before. Perhaps he shared with him how God's power had been made perfect in weakness. He would have talked with him about his failures as well as his successes. Above all he would have encouraged Elisha to walk closely with the Lord, to seek His face alone, to stake his life on the Word of God alone, and to listen and obey.

How to receive the "full portion" of the Holy Spirit

How, then, did Elisha receive his full portion, the complete anointing, of the Holy Spirit? How can God's people today experience the baptism with the Holy Spirit that only Jesus can give? He had to do three things, the very three things Jesus told His disciples to do. *"Ask, and it will be given to you; seek, and you will find; knock, and it will be opened to you. For everyone who asks receives, and the one who seeks finds, and to the one who knocks it will be opened."* Jesus added, *"If you then, who are evil, know how to give good gifts to your children, how much more will the heavenly Father give the Holy Spirit to those who ask Him!"* (Luke 11:9-13)

Ask. Ten years of learning had not been enough for Elisha. For many missionaries today, ten years of laboring under difficult circumstances is not enough to be effective in changing a nation. Faithful church attendance and much reading of the Bible is not enough. We must *ask for the baptism with the Holy Spirit!* And we must ask the one Person who gives it: Jesus. Remember! Everyone who asks receives.

Seek. But it is not enough to ask. Elijah said to Elisha, *"If you see me as I am being taken from you, it shall be so for you."* Elisha had to watch and pray. Jesus tells His disciples in all times and situations, "Abide in Me! Seek My face!" We do not receive the infilling of the Holy Spirit automatically. Although the Spirit lives inside every believer, we must ask Jesus, yielding every area of our lives to Him; we must fix our gaze upon Him alone, if we are to receive the empowering of His Spirit. We must keep our eyes on Jesus alone.

Knock. Elisha had asked; he saw Elijah being taken up into heaven. Now there was only one thing left to do. He had to *take* what had been offered to him. He had to make it his own, to receive wholeheartedly the gift that God was giving to him. This demanded an action on Elisha's part, not just a passive acceptance. Many people ask for the gift of the Holy Spirit. They even try to keep their eyes on Jesus and focus their lives on Him. Yet they do not become filled with the Holy Spirit. This is because they passively expect God to perform the miracle of sending the empowering Spirit into their lives without any aggressive action of receiving on their part. Some people hang their heads low in a seemingly contrite pose as if the Spirit would come and lift them up with a mighty wind. But we must *make it our own, with great, expectant joy!* It requires a spirit of "humble boldness" to take what is being offered. Elisha struck the water saying, *"Where is the Lord, the God of Elijah?"* The waters were parted and he crossed over.

New leaders must learn to *ask.* We must live by prayer, which is the Christian's vital breath, or we will never be true leaders sent by God. We have nothing in ourselves; everything is in God. We live in complete dependence on God. *"In everything by prayer and supplication with thanksgiving let your requests be made known to God."* (Philippians 4:6)

New leaders must learn to *seek.* A leader must become a *contemplative* person, as King David was: *"I saw the Lord always before me, for He is at my right hand that I may not be shaken."* (Acts 2:25) We must walk with Jesus, with our eyes on Him, worshiping as we walk and as we work.

Finally, new leaders must learn to *knock.* We must receive all the Lord gives us. And we must test out the many gifts and make sure they work in our lives. Elisha did that, and it worked. The Lord is happy when His people challenge Him by faith to be true to His Word. We must learn to live as Elijah and Elisha lived, obeying God in all that He commands us to do and trusting Him to do all we cannot do.

Questions for Further Thought and Discussion
Please read 2 Kings 2:1-15
before answering these questions.

1. Do you see evidence of the "spirit of Jezebel" in society today? What are some examples? In light of this, what kind of young leaders would you like to see arise to change the world? If you are a young, potential leader, how will you respond to Jesus' call on your life?

2. We have said that two key issues involved in transferring leadership from the older to the younger generation are *continuity* and *letting go of authority*. How can we reconcile these two seemingly contradictory issues?

3. Have you personally received a "double portion"—that is, the full portion to which you are entitled as a child of God—of the Holy Spirit who worked in Elijah? If not, are you seeking the baptism, or infilling, of the Holy Spirit? Why not pray now that God will answer your prayer and fill you to overflowing with His Holy Spirit!

Notes

The Baptism With the Holy Spirit

The Four Gospels introduce Jesus Christ both as the Lamb of God who takes away the sin of the world and as the one who baptizes with the Holy Spirit. (John 1:29-33)

Weakness in our lives and ministry drives us to seek the power of the Holy Spirit. We do not want to be weak. So we are surprised when the Holy Spirit, who fills us with His great power, then reveals to us how weak and totally helpless we are. The baptism with the Holy Spirit does not cause us to "possess" power; rather, it enables us to rejoice in our weaknesses so that the power of God may be manifested in our lives. God does not tolerate our moral weaknesses; we must repent, turn away from our sins and be forgiven. But He rejoices greatly when we realize that we are destitute and have no power, and then seek *His* power, which Paul says is "made perfect in our weakness." (2 Corinthians 12:9)

Are you ready to be baptized with the Holy Spirit? Using the word "ready" as an acrostic, let us seek the gift that will enable us to be God's nation changers.

R—Repent; turn away from all sin, from all unhealthy relations and from anything in your life that you consider more important than God. Receive God's forgiveness by faith.

E—Expect; wait in confident trust and expectation that Jesus will baptize you with His Holy Spirit, as He has promised. Expect the Holy Spirit to come to you as fire, burning away all that has bound you, igniting your heart with a burning passion to love Jesus alone, and creating His warmth within you that will cause you to pursue peace and unity with all other believers.

A—Ask; be specific in your request. Do not ask for other things at this time, only that Jesus will send the Father's promised Holy Spirit.

D—Drink; accept Jesus' invitation in John 7:37-38: *"If anyone thirsts, let him come to Me and drink. Whoever believes in Me, as the Scripture has said, 'Out of his heart will flow rivers of living water.'"*

Y—Yield; give full control of your life to God, yielding to His Spirit's gentle power as He begins to take complete control of your whole life.

Chapter Ten

Beginning a New Ministry: Blessing and Curse
2 Kings 2:15-25

⟨❈⟩

*E*lisha began his ministry with boldness, not simply with human self-confidence. He was no more confident than his teacher Elijah had been. But he shared Elijah's boldness. Biblical boldness is to tremble before the Lord and His Word, in humility and obedience. The one who trembles before God's Word trusts in God and not in himself. Boldness comes from the confidence that God will never forsake or leave His own, and that He will do everything He has promised to do. *"The people who know their God shall stand firm and take action."* (Daniel 11:32) For those who are willing to be instruments in God's hand, God works wonders among the nations.

This passage is an account of the first days of Elisha's ministry, the launching of his service to the Lord. His beginning was full of blessings but also doubt and even a curse. This was to be a somewhat rocky beginning of the ministry of a prophet who later became known for more miracles connected with his ministry than anyone else, except Jesus Christ.

Boldness was inherent in Elisha's calling. When Elijah first called Elisha to follow him, he threw his cloak upon Elisha. This was a sign of God's favor and a sign that Elisha also would walk in the power of the Spirit just as his forerunner Elijah had done. Later, at the end of Elijah's ministry, when he took Elisha with him across the Jordan, Elijah took his cloak and struck the waters; the Jordan River was parted from one side to the other, and they walked across on dry ground. Now the time had come for Elisha to show his bold faith in the Lord. It was not enough that Elijah had thrown his cloak upon Elisha, or that Elijah had shown his power to Elisha by throwing his cloak on the waters. Now Elisha had to *pick up Elijah's mantle and use it.* When he did so, the Spirit of the Lord came upon him in boldness, and the Jordan River parted once again. He never had to depend on Elijah again! He followed in the footsteps of Joshua, who had been as certain of God's leading and power as his teacher Moses had been.

The sign of Jesus' presence

We may see many signs that confirm God's acknowledgment of us as His servants. But we need only one sign: Jesus Christ's *presence* in our midst, through the inner working of the Holy Spirit who *"bears witness with our spirit that we are children of God."* (Romans 8:16) Through Him we cry out, "Abba! Father!" Those who long for God's presence, who seek His face each morning and turn their ear to listen to all He wants to say in His Word know that we need no other sign. Intimacy with the Lord is the greatest joy of their life.

When we enjoy daily intimacy with Jesus, we become aware of His greatest promise, which is to baptize us with His Holy Spirit! The Spirit works in the lives of Christians today just as He worked in the Early Church. *"God also bore witness by signs and wonders and various miracles and by gifts of the Holy Spirit distributed according to His will."* (Hebrews 2:4) Perhaps the greatest of all signs given to God's people today is the perfect peace and unity that God grants to us when we love one another just as Christ has loved us.

The presence of God! For Elisha, this was the goal of his life! This was also the goal of the psalmist when he wrote, *"I have set the Lord always before me; because He is at my right hand, I shall not be shaken."* (Psalm 16:8) His presence gives not only power and gifts for ministry, but also a peace that the world does not know, joy even in suffering, certainty in our faith, consolation in times of loss, and enlightenment when we walk through dark valleys.

The "sons of the prophets" were prophets in training, similar to today's young Bible school or theological seminary students preparing for ministry. This group in Elisha's day had no experience of God; they had only "studied" about him and had watched the power of Elijah. The students of this school of the prophets urged Elisha to seek for Elijah. Perhaps the Lord was hiding him somewhere. They urged Elisha "till he was ashamed." They could not believe Elijah was truly gone. They still could not believe that Elisha was prepared for the task. There was doubt in the community of believers, doubt that has been carried down even to the present day. Every new leader has to confront this doubt. Joseph, the one true prophet in his family, had to face doubt from his brothers, who considered him to be a dreamer and a deceiver.

The deception of beauty

The city leaders of Jericho were proud of their city and lauded its beauty to young Elisha. Jericho was, from all outward appearances, a beautiful city. Its natural situation was ideal; the best architects had built it. But there was a deep irony in their boasting about their city. They were deceived because of the outward beauty of Jericho. "Our city is beautiful," they said to Elisha, "but we have a problem." Their problem was that the water in the spring that fed the wells was poisoned by some hidden and deep source of pollution, and *no one could solve the problem!* The poison caused miscarriages among both people and cattle, and they could not grow good crops.

The same could be said of some of the most beautiful cities in the world today. They have everything—wonderful culture, varieties of religion, high standards of living. But the *spring of life* has been poisoned! Something is wrong at the very heart of many of our cities—greed, political and economic corruption, anti-God educational systems, sex trafficking, child pornography, to mention only a few. The world we live in is a very beautiful world, except for the concentration camps, the child brothels, the extreme poverty, famine, or the senseless murdering of children in schools around the world.

Jericho was almost to the point where people would have to abandon the city. There were those who probably remembered the curse God had placed upon the city during the days of Joshua. (Joshua 6:26) They may have felt that this curse was now visiting its present inhabitants. Others believed there were evil spirits in the wells. Basically, the problem was the *human situation*. It was a city without God. Today we face the same problem of reconstruction of human society that Elisha faced.

Elisha's solution

Elisha's solution was twofold. He used both a sign and a word to solve the problem. The sign was salt. Salt was used in religious rites of separation, as when a priest was separated in order to be purified. The priest was being separated from the common to join with the sacred. When Elisha threw salt into the spring of water, he was performing a ritual of purification of the water. This spring existed to give life to the city of Jericho, but instead it was giving death. Elisha was now separating the poison and death and consecrating this water to be holy. The city would no longer be cursed but rather would receive a blessing.

But it was not the new bowl of salt that purified the city; that was merely a sign. The Word of the Lord is what healed and purified the city! *"Thus says the Lord, 'I have healed this water; from now on neither death nor miscarriage shall come from it.' So the water has been healed to this day, according to the word that Elisha spoke."* (2 Kings 2:21-22) How true the Word of the Lord is! When we visited the city of Jericho in 1972, we were able to drink from that very same spring of water that God healed! It was still as pure as it was in the days of Elisha.

"Thus says the Lord!" It was the Word, not the sign, that brought life to the city. God's Word puts life into His signs! All the signs and miracles of the Bible point to the Word of God! What does the Church have to say to modern problems of pollution, of environmental destruction? What does the Church today have to say to the problem of the very rich getting much richer, and the very poor getting much poorer? What does the Church have to say to national and regional problems such as the rebuilding of North Korea? Do we simply continue preaching the Gospel of individual salvation and neglect

social and national sins? Do we simply build replicas of our own church buildings, or more seminaries to train pastors and leaders like ourselves? By no means! We can and must point to the only solution. *When the Word of God is proclaimed faithfully and truly in a nation, or a city, God will bring restoration to that nation or city!* The Word of God brings social miracles as well as spiritual miracles.

Bethel and Jericho

Elisha continued on to the city of Bethel, where he learned another hard lesson during those first days of ministry. He learned that his word could bring judgment and damnation as well as blessing and life. We must look at the first days as a whole. The city of Jericho had been cursed by God, but now the people of the city turned back to the Word of God in their need. The city of Bethel was where Abraham built one of his first altars to worship God and where God renewed His covenant with Jacob. It was here that Jacob had had his vision of the heavenly ladder with the angels of God descending and ascending upon it. But after many years, the people of Bethel had now turned away from worshiping God. There is evidence that Baal worship was prominent in Bethel. So the people of Bethel had become *enemies of God.* The adults had taught their children and young people well, but they did not teach them to worship God. Rather, they had taught them to turn away from God and to mock the prophets of the Lord.

The dark side of power

Most scholars agree that the "small boys" mentioned in our text probably do not refer to small boys or children at all. Rather, they were very likely roving bands of young boys and men very similar to what we see today. In nations around the world today we hear of middle school students viciously attacking elderly or disabled people, or of young boys murdering homeless people; we read in our newspapers of high school students massacring other students in acts of violence. So these were not just small children mocking Elisha's baldness; they were young men who had learned from their parents to hate God. *"Go up, you baldhead!"* may have referred to the ascension of Elijah, telling Elisha to try to do the same thing. Just as is often the case today, the youth of the city of Bethel were the actual spokesmen for the city itself!

Nevertheless, Elisha's actions were inexcusable, and we cannot defend them. We see here one of the tragic misuses of power. We see the dark side of power, rather than the light side. Jesus did not curse people, and Elisha was wrong to curse. Jesus told the Pharisees, "I do not judge you; you have judged yourselves."

We are reminded, however, that the Gospel contains an element of judgment. Paul said, *"We are the aroma of Christ to God among those who are being saved and among those who are perishing, to one a fragrance from death to death, to the other a fragrance from life to life."* (2 Corinthians 2:15-16) Jesus Himself said, *"For judgment I came into this world, that those who do not see may see, and that those who see may become blind."* (John 9:39) The fire that purifies and cleanses is also the fire that consumes.

The reversal of the two cities' fortunes was astounding. Jericho was a city God had cursed many years before, and Bethel was a place God had blessed. Now, God was reversing their fortunes through Elisha. God's grace is free to all, but it is not automatic. Certain places or people groups may flourish for a time under God's grace but then turn away and reject Him. Nations, as well as individuals, must choose to remain under the blessing of God or under the curse.

Free from curses

Today many people and nations have made the choice to live under the curse rather than the blessing. But those who belong to the Kingdom of Jesus Christ are free from curses. Curses are not transmitted from one generation to the next, nor do they remain forever upon a certain people or place. The blood of Jesus Christ breaks every curse that may have come to us in the past or that comes upon us in the present. We must decide to trust God, with full confidence that He will not allow us to be destroyed by Satan. The moment to decide to accept the grace of God comes to each person, and to each nation. God is a God of the *present* and not just the past. The throne room of heaven is wide open to all who will enter.

After this rather rocky beginning, Elisha went on to Mount Carmel, very likely determined to seek God once again to understand this awesome, terrible power that had come upon him. From there he continued on to Samaria to continue his ministry as servant of the Lord.

Questions for Thought and Discussion
Please read 2 Kings 2:15-25
before answering these questions.

1. What is the sign or signs in your life that reveal that God is working both in you and through you to change the world?

2. What is the spiritual condition of the city in which you live? How do you think God wants to use you to cleanse your city? What steps are you taking to see the Kingdom of God advance in your city or nation?

3. We have seen, through Elisha's ordeal with the young men who mocked him, that power has both a light and dark side. Can you see evidence of this in your nation? Read Philippians 2:14-16 and consider how we, as the people of God, can demonstrate true spiritual power and authority in the world.

Notes

Christians and Curses

Curses are not passed down from generation to generation on Christians who have been washed clean by the blood of Jesus Christ. Galatians 3:13 tells us that Christ has redeemed us from the curse of the law by becoming a curse for us. Because we have been freed from the curse of the law, we now live under the grace of God that sets us free. All the blessings of God are in Christ and received by faith. However, if we do not walk in faith but choose to live under the law, with all its rules, regulations and demands, we remain under a curse. This means that it is indeed possible for Christians who walk away from their salvation in Christ, who reject living by faith alone and go back to the old life of trying to work hard to please God by the things they do, to place themselves once again under the curse of the law.

Some Christian teachers today teach that curses are passed on from generation to generation, even for Christians who walk by faith. But a careful examination of their teaching shows that they depend almost entirely on Old Testament passages, certainly none from the New Testament. This kind of teaching is not the "Great Gospel" of which the writer of Hebrews speaks. The victory comes not from popular teachers who offer to pray to "lift the generational curses" from Christians. Christians are removed from curses by the shed blood of Jesus Christ, the blood of the New Covenant. True knowledge of God frees us from all curses. Abiding in God's Word leads us into truth. Jesus said, *"You will know the truth, and the truth will set you free."* (John 8:32)

Satan continues to attack born-again Christians. Satanic groups and individuals place curses on Christians even today. But we must remember that we are not only washed clean by the shed blood of Jesus Christ, we are also covered by that blood. Satan is a murderer and the father of lies. He works by deception. We must care for one another, pray for one another and confront Satan with the truth—in the name of Jesus, by the power of the Holy Spirit, using the weapon of the blood—to resist him. Then the devil must flee. (James 4:7) We must decide to rejoice in our salvation, to live by faith in obedience to God's will, and to resist the attacks of the enemy with full confidence that no weapon of Satan that is fashioned against us shall succeed.

Chapter Eleven

The Makings of a Miracle
2 Kings 4:1-7

𝄞

*G*od does not visit only houses of congress or parliament. He does not merely direct the affairs of nations. He is also the God of each individual living in the world. He controls the destiny of rulers and nations, but He also cares for the widow and the orphan. The Apostle James defines God's view of true religion: *"Religion that is pure and undefiled before God, the Father, is this: to visit orphans and widows in their affliction, and to keep oneself unstained from the world."* (James 1:27)

"Who is like the Lord our God, who is seated on high, who looks far down on the heavens and the earth? He raises the poor from the dust and lifts the needy from the ash heap." (Psalm 113:5-7) *God comes to those who call upon Him. He is a well-proven help in times of trouble. He desires to meet us in His throne room at the beginning of each day, to renew us through His mercy and compassion and to pour out His grace upon us in all times of need.*

Elijah and Elisha were like their Master, God; they were accessible to individual people, both rich and poor, not just to leaders of the nation. They had great influence in their nation, and many young men sought to be trained by them, hoping to be endowed with the spiritual gift of prophecy that God had given to Elijah and Elisha. Had these young men known the full cost of being a prophet of the Lord, such as Elijah had paid, or in later times Isaiah, Jeremiah, Ezekiel and Hosea would have to pay, perhaps they would have been more reticent in their longing to be prophets. Old Testament prophets did not merely give a word of prophecy and then separate themselves from their people, as some modern day prophets do. On the contrary, Elijah and Elisha, as well as Jeremiah and Ezekiel, were deeply involved in the lives of the people they served.

A prophetic community emerged, centered on Elijah and Elisha. Micaiah was one of them (1 Kings 22), and there were other young men who became part of the community to learn from Elijah and Elisha. Some of these "sons of the prophets," as they were called, were married. And we learn from Scripture that there was no provision for their widows after a husband's death. A young widow came crying to Elisha with a story of injustice. Her husband had died, and through no fault of her own she had been forced to incur debt in order to survive. The social system of Elisha's day was so corrupt that welfare provisions in Moses' law were ignored. They knew the law but chose to disobey it. Leviticus 25:39-41 states that a fellow Israelite could not be taken as a slave to repay a debt, but that the person in debt would receive wages from the lender while working to repay it. However, this widow reported to Elisha that the creditor had come to take her two children as slaves until she repaid the debt.

"What shall I do for you?"

Elisha's immediate response was to ask the widow a question: *"What shall I do for you?"* His question revealed his pastoral heart. This is a question Christians should ask one another daily: "Is there anything I can do to help you? What can I do for you?" When we ask one another this question, we are beginning to have the mind of Christ. To go one step further, when we as the Church of Jesus Christ ask this question to the neglected poor in society, we are practicing true religion. When Jesus saw the blind beggar Bartimaeus, his first question was, *"What do you want me to do for you?"* (Mark 10:51)

God is accessible to us today also. He is near to us, and He continually asks us what He can do for us. When we read and study, or meditate upon His Word, He comes to us. When we gather around the Lord's table at holy communion, He reveals Himself to us in a fresh way. Whenever we call upon His name, He is there to meet our needs.

"What do you have?"

Elisha asked one more question: *"What have you in the house?"* Her answer was, "Nothing." Yet she did have a few things. She had a *jar of oil.* She also, like her deceased husband, had the *"fear of the Lord."* The Bible defines the "fear of the Lord" as standing before the Word of God with trembling and humility, and allowing that Word to break us and then remold us into the image of Jesus Christ. Jesus hates sin and loves righteousness, and that is the heart of one who fears the Lord. The fear of the Lord increases expectation that God will act. So this widow had many more things than she thought. In addition to the jar of oil and the fear of the Lord, she had *expectant faith* to look to

God in her need. She knew she had no resources in herself to meet her needs, but she was willing to obey by placing all that she had at God's disposal, so that He could do as He wished. She had felt that the jar of oil was nothing, but she now came to realize that God could use it to meet her needs. This widow would have clearly understood what Mary, the mother of Jesus, meant when she told the servants, *"Do whatever He tells you."* (John 2:5)

"Go, borrow vessels from all your neighbors."

God used more than her dependence on Him to meet her needs. He also used her neighbors to deliver her from her poverty. We often prefer God to come to us personally when we have a need, rather than having to humble ourselves to ask our neighbors for help. The Apostle Paul must have been surprised when God sent Ananias to pray for him after his experience on the road to Damascus. But God actually used the unknown man Ananias to inaugurate Paul's ministry. God called him to pray that Paul (Saul) would regain his sight and be filled with the Holy Spirit. Even Jesus welcomed the comfort and encouragement of His friends Lazarus, Mary and Martha. Jesus knew that their friendship was a gift from His Father in heaven, and He visited them often.

Every Christian is called to minister to others, and a spirit of generosity greatly strengthens our ministry. We must be neighbors to all who need our help, regardless of their religion, their politics or their social standing. But this passage reminds us that we also must be ready to accept help for our needs from others. This is a privilege and blessing we must never abuse by expecting other people to meet all our needs. We must be willing to ask when we are in need, but more willing to give to others beyond our ability to give.

". . . and not too few."

Elisha knew that the widow might have been hesitant to ask for many empty containers from her neighbors. He also knew that she probably did not expect that she would need that many. So he said, *". . . and not too few."* We limit God by our unbelief. God wanted to provide more for this widow than she was prepared to accept. He was telling her to enlarge her faith. Our faith so often stops before God's grace is finished! How much more God could do! How much more greatly God could use us if we were to trust Him completely. The famous Scottish Bible expositor Alexander Maclaren once said that "God keeps giving Himself as long as we bring ourselves as empty vessels into which He can pour Himself. . . . He cannot give the oil unless we bring the vessels of our hearts opened by our desires. You have God in the measure in which you desire Him."[12]

The motto of William Carey's life was: "Expect great things from God. Attempt great things for God!" We may add one thing to this: Think great thoughts for God! When we know Him as He truly is, our minds and hearts are enlarged; our faith increases. Not only will we receive more when we expect great things from God; more importantly, we can *do more* to alleviate suffering in our neighbors' lives and in the world, and to proclaim the Gospel of reconciliation with power.

"Shut the door behind yourself."

God worked His mighty miracle behind closed doors. The neighbors could not watch the multiplication of oil that filled all their empty vessels. They never knew how much their gift of one little container helped the widow and her sons. This is often true in lives as well. We may never know how much the cup of cold water that we gave to one who was thirsty helped him. It may have changed his life.

This is part of the *hiddenness* of faith. Our lives have been rescued, or healed, or shaped by countless people who have prayed for us. Someone may have given a gift in our time of need. We have only to be thankful, and to be content in being hidden ourselves as we minister to the people God sends our way. Elijah may have told her to shut the door in order to preserve her dignity. He undoubtedly did it so that God alone would receive all the glory.

"Go, sell the oil and pay your debts, and. . . live."

With one simple act of faith, the widow's debt was wiped away. We rejoice that Jesus Christ, by His one act of substitution on the cross, wiped away our debt of sin and freed us from bondage and fear. *"For the death He died He died to sin, once for all."* (Romans 6:10)

But we must not stop here. Jesus tells us that He not only saves us from sin but also saves us to fullness of life in Him. *"I came that they may have life and have it abundantly."* (John 10:10) The widow became wealthy enough from the oil to live comfortably with her family for the rest of her life. Having been blessed by God, through His people, she became a source of blessing to her neighbors. We have the promise: *"And God is able to make all grace abound to you, so that having all sufficiency in all things at all times, you may abound in every good work."* (2 Corinthians 9:8)

Questions for Thought and Discussion
Please read 2 Kings 4:1-7
before answering these questions.

1. Have you ever heard Jesus say directly to you, "What do you want Me to do for you?" What were the circumstances surrounding you when He visited you with His offer to help? Describe what happened when you responded to Him.

2. How has God supplied your needs over the past few years? Has He done so by giving you a job, or by directly supplying all that you need? Has He used other people to minister to your needs? What role has generosity played in your finances?

3. Why do you think Elisha told the widow to go inside her house and shut the door behind herself and her two sons in order to experience the miracle? Would you have preferred to see the miracle happen publicly as a testimony to God's faithfulness? Do you think there is too much emphasis placed on the public display of God's miracle-working power? Which of the two ways would encourage you personally to be willing to allow God to work a miracle through you?

Notes

The Fear of the Lord and the Miraculous

Rulers of nations, both good and evil, fear God. But theirs is not a holy fear, rather a deep anxiety that stems from their awareness that God is all-powerful and that He alone controls the rise and fall of world leaders.

But there is a holy fear, and the Bible calls it the *fear of the Lord.* The young widow told Elisha that she and her husband feared the Lord. The fear of the Lord provides the foundation for miracles. The Acts of the Apostles records that the Early Church was filled with the fear of the Lord. *"And awe came upon every soul, and many wonders and signs were being done through the apostles."* (Acts 2:43) The same word in Greek can be translated as both *fear* and *awe.* Fear of the Lord led to great miracles, signs and wonders in the Early Church; it will do the same today.

The psalmist says that the Word of God itself is the fear of the Lord. (Psalm 19:9) The fear of the Lord means to stand before the Word of God in humility and with a contrite spirit, trembling before the Word. (Isaiah 66:2) When we allow that Word to break us and lead us to turn away from all sin and turn toward the Lord with a heart committed to loving only what He loves and hating all He hates, then we will know the fear of the Lord. Proverbs 2:1-5 shows us the way:

"My son, if you receive my words and treasure up my commandments with you, making your ear attentive to wisdom and inclining your heart to understanding; yes, if you call out for insight and raise your voice for understanding, if you seek it like silver and search for it as for hidden treasures, then you will understand the fear of the Lord and find the knowledge of God."

The psalmist wisely links praising the Lord with the fear of the Lord, for only as we fear the Lord and turn away from evil can we freely, and fully, praise the Lord. Together these two things—fear of the Lord and praising the Lord—lead to great blessings in the Christian life. The psalmist even tells us that *the angel of the Lord encamps around those who fear Him, and delivers them."* (Ps. 34:7)

Chapter Twelve

Faith That Rebels
2 Kings 4:8-37; 8:1-6

❦

We come now to another major miracle that took place under Elisha's ministry, only this time the great faith that was required came not only from Elisha but also from the woman he was helping. She started out with very little faith but in the end portrayed a faith that rebelled against Satan's evil plans. Hers is a story of the building of one's faith to be ready for the miraculous works of God. D.S. Cairns says that the miracles of God teach us "that God is more near, more real and mighty, more full of love and more ready to help every one of us than any one of us realizes! This," he says, "is the underlying message of miracles."

A godly woman of Shunem showed great kindness to Elisha. She had noticed him passing by her house frequently, and she opened her home to him as a place of rest from his journeys. She and her husband prepared a small room on the flat roof of their house. Although her husband was elderly, Elisha prophesied that she would have a son, and his prophecy came to pass. But when the child was grown he died suddenly, and God used Elisha to bring him back to life.

The prophet's chamber

In those days such a room was called a "prophet's chamber." It had simple furnishings: a bed, a chair, a table and a lamp stand, the bare essentials for living. This revealed another mark of both Elijah's and Elisha's lifestyle, a simplicity in living that enabled them to better perform the Lord's work.

This room became Elisha's place of prayer and rest, and the place where a miracle would take place. The Shunammite woman sensed Elisha's needs and practiced her gift of hospitality. Little did she know that her gift to Elisha would set the stage for a miracle, just as at a later time Mary's and Martha's gift of hospitality would result in the miracle of the raising of Lazarus! *"The one who receives a prophet because he is a prophet will receive a prophet's reward, and the one who receives a righteous person because he is a righteous person will receive a righteous person's reward."* (Matthew 10:41) Perhaps this is why the New Testament emphasizes the gift of hospitality as being so important. One of Paul's last exhortations to the Christians in Rome was, *"Contribute to the needs of the saints and seek to show hospitality."* (Romans 12:13) Hospitality means to see every person as if that person were Jesus, and to serve that person in love.

Elisha, like many Christians who serve others today, was more accustomed to doing something for others than accepting what they wanted to do for him. So he offered to repay her. Elisha seemed to be more comfortable approaching her through his servant Gehazi. He offered to use his influence with the king to speak to him on her behalf; perhaps there was something she needed

for her family. But she refused. Her response was digni-
fied: *"I dwell among my own people."* This meant she was
perfectly content with her situation as it was and had
no ambitions for anything greater. Elisha was revealing
a somewhat worldly attitude here, but the woman was
stately in letting him know that she was secure and very
content in her lifestyle. Above all, she showed the true
spirit of hospitality: She was serving the prophet *because
of his need,* not in order to later get a blessing or benefit
from him.

The promise of the Word of God

Elisha told his servant Gehazi to find out what she
needed; he reported back to Elisha that she was childless
and unable to have children. Elijah gave her a promise,
that at the same time the following year she would have
a son! This would be a beautiful gift, one that would bring
great blessing to her home.

But her response was, *"O man of God, do not lie to your
servant!"* Without a doubt she had dreamed of having a
son but knew that it was impossible. She had decided
to not think about it. She may have felt that Elisha was
mocking her, trying to revive her old disappointments, or
reminding her of her reproach. In the Middle East at that
time childlessness was regarded as a stigma, a reproach
from God.

Yet the prophecy disturbed her. She had a deep desire,
a longing for a son, but could not believe it was possible.
So she sadly repressed her desire and forced herself to
be content. When Elisha spoke the word of prophecy to
her, she rejected it at first, because she could not bear
being disappointed again. Nevertheless, Elisha's word
disturbed her "disappointed contentment." She could not
understand it. She did not ask for a son, in fact she would

never have considered doing so. But the Word of the Lord was *thrust upon her.* At the same time it disturbed her, it also created a new expectation and aroused her faith! This Word from the Lord caused her to begin to dream again of new possibilities and of the richness of God!

What is the role of the Word of God in developing a community of faith? From this story we can discover five lessons about faith and the Word of God.

First, the Word of God creates faith. *"So faith comes from hearing, and hearing through the Word of Christ."* (Romans 10:17) We are not talking about just hearing the words of the Bible read. We are talking about the power of the Word when God speaks directly to us through His Word. In the midst of this woman's sad resignation to her childlessness, God's Word to her through Elisha made her suddenly come alive! This seemingly absurd promise from God would change her life forever!

When the Word of God comes to us, it may seem to be so impossible of fulfillment that we refuse to take it seriously. But God's Word promises that *in spite of the impossibilities,* we can be changed. God can take away our reproach; He can remove our unfruitfulness.

When the great missionary Adoniram Judson was bound in chains in a Burmese jail, the other prisoners mocked him saying, "What are the prospects of your converting the heathen now?" His reply was, "The prospects are as bright as the promises of God!" There are no impossibilities with God, neither are there any failures in Him. We must not interpret the Bible in a way that minimizes the miracles God wants to do in our lives.

God's promises will come as we abide in His Word! Charles Spurgeon, often called the "preacher of preachers," said that Jesus' words of "all power has been given unto Me.... I am with you always" create faith that leads to infinite possibilities. He told his people that we should not say, "I will do what I can." Anybody can do that, he said. Rather we must say, "I will do what I cannot do, I will trust God and attempt the impossible!"[14]

Elizabeth said of Mary, *"Blessed is she who believed that there would be a fulfillment of what was spoken to her from the Lord."* (Luke 1:45) The Shunammite woman was beginning her journey of faith. But she was to learn yet another lesson.

Second, faith rebels against Satan's plan to destroy God's promises. The woman conceived and bore a child, just as Elisha had spoken. But when the child had grown, he was working one morning with his father on the farm when his head began to hurt terribly. His mother held him in her lap until noon, and he died.

The mother reacted in a strange way. It would have been natural to prepare him for burial and mourn, and say, "The Lord gave and the Lord takes away." Instead she took up her son to the prophet's chamber and laid him on Elisha's bed. She shut the door and went out.

This child was God's gift to her when she was unable to bear a child. Our Scripture does not tell us how she knew, but it seems probable that she had received a word of comfort from the Lord during her grieving that made her think her son would live again. She informed her husband that she was going to see the prophet. When he questioned why, she only said, *"All is well."* She was becoming bolder in her faith. She departed for Mount Carmel to meet Elisha.

Elisha saw her coming and told his servant to ask her if everything was well with her son. Her reply was, *"All is well."* All was not well with her son; he was dead. But *all was well with her soul!* She had learned, as the Apostle Paul was later to learn, that in whatever circumstance we find ourselves, in plenty or in want, in sickness or in health, even when tragedy strikes, we can be secure and content in God's love. God is still in control!

The hymn writer expresses it most beautifully:

> *When peace, like a river, attendeth my way,*
> *when sorrows like sea billows roll;*
> *whatever my lot, Thou hast taught me to say,*
> *It is well, it is well with my soul.*
>
> Words by Horatio G. Spafford
> Music by Philip P. Bliss

Her contentment was not resignation to a hopeless situation. Rather, her contentment in the Lord gave her boldness to grab hold of Elisha's feet and refuse to leave until she received *everything God had promised her!* Hers was a faith that rebelled against Satan's evil plans. She used Elijah's and Elisha's own words, in saying, *"As the Lord lives and as you yourself live, I will not leave you!"* She was saying, "You and your God will have to solve this problem!"

Third, faith presses in until God fulfills His promises. This woman knew well and was practicing what Isaiah would later say: *"You who put the Lord in remembrance, take no rest, and give Him no rest until He establishes Jerusalem and makes it a praise in the earth."* (Isaiah 62:6-7) She was persistent and single-minded in her faith.

Fourth, compassion is an essential ingredient of faith. Compassion means to enter into others' suffering, taking their pain upon ourselves and then going together with them to the cross of Jesus Christ for healing and life. Professor Ronald S. Wallace once said to our class of students who were eagerly listening to his teaching on this subject, "Perhaps we have to learn that the Church of Christ is built by our tears as well as by our work." Elisha's ministry to the Shunammite woman was completed only when he sacrificed his time and energy for the son and was *willing to enter into the suffering and the pain of the death of this young man!*

Fifth, the fulfillment of the Word depends on genuine intercession and sacrifice. Elisha entered into this family's suffering through the ministry of genuine intercession and sacrifice on their behalf. He had to give up all his dignity and share the great grief of this family, suffering along with them. By interceding in prayer, Elisha was able to give this suffering to his Lord rather than taking it upon himself. His Lord was the Suffering Servant who takes away the sins and grief of the world.

We must continue to believe, and to commit our lives to this end, that the Kingdom of God can break into every situation we face today. The Bible teaches that God not only saves the soul but that He is available to bring changes in our lives each day. Elisha's prayer for the young man was a foreshadowing of the sacrifice of Jesus Christ, and of His prayer in the Garden of Gethsemane.

The result was the resurrection of the dead son. He simply said to the mother, *"Take your son."* (2 Kings 4:37) But this family's story does not end here. Shortly after this miracle, Elisha told her that the Lord had called for a famine that would last seven years and advised her family to seek refuge in another country. When the family returned after seven years, someone had usurped their property. While the king was talking with Gehazi, Elisha's servant (who must have been healed from his leprosy), about the mighty deeds of Elisha, the woman suddenly appeared. When the king saw her, he not only restored her property but also provided her with all the income she would have received from her land had she remained in the country. (2 Kings 8:1-6)

Situations today may not have this same happy ending. We might not receive our deceased loved ones back again through resurrection; we might not receive the justice due to us in financial matters. But even if our own stories do not have this happy ending, we know that the God of love is still working in our lives and throughout the world. We trust Him who works all things together for good, to work out His perfect will in our lives.

Questions for Further Thought and Discussion
Please read 2 Kings 4:8-37
before answering these questions.

1. Are you able to receive fully and freely the hospitality and generosity of others as their true gift to you? Or do you feel that you must in some way repay them for their service to you? If so, then when you serve others do you look for them to "repay" you for your generosity? Describe the heart of the Shunammite woman as you understand her.

2. Review the development of the Shunammite woman's faith. Perhaps she urged her husband to build a "prophet's chamber" on their flat roof patio with the hope that she and her husband would both help Elisha and also grow in their faith. What were the elements that caused her faith to grow to the extent that she could confess "All is well!" even when her son died, and then to expect his resurrection? What were some of the ways God has increased your own faith?

3. Elisha was a man of compassion. The word comes from the Latin prefix *com,* meaning "with," and the Latin word *passion,* which means "suffering." Elisha was willing to share the sufferings of his people. What do you think Ronald S. Wallace meant when he told his students, "Perhaps we have to learn that the Church of Christ is built by our tears as well as by our work"? Do you agree? Is compassion a mark of your life?

Notes

The Faith That Rebels

D.S. Cairns, in his remarkable book *The Faith That Rebels,* [15] speaks of the intellectual dual between those who accept and those who reject miracles. He maintains that his study of the Synoptic Gospels led him to see that there was more in the teachings of Jesus on "the power of faith and the range of prayer than were finding expression in our current Christian thought and practice." He says that there is something in the teaching of Jesus that is not finding an adequate expression in our current theological and religious teaching. Words spoken nearly one hundred years ago still ring true today.

Cairns says that Jesus' constant call for faith in God was in effect Him saying, "I have brought the Kingdom of God and all its blessings within your reach. It is for you to take it by faith."[16] Jesus' summons to faith remains absolute. The world of nature, in comparison with God, has no power. God alone is Lord of all creation.

There remains the problem of evil. Cairns continues by asking why it was that the Protestant churches of the Reformation were so slow in attempting to evangelize the world. He answers by saying that it was because they accepted "heathenism" as a great immovable mountain that was blocking the Kingdom of God. Cairns' main thesis is that Christians must not accept limits to the power and love of God and the possibilities of faith. Rather, we must "rebel" against the power of evil that seeks to make Christians feel that they are defenseless against Satan's assaults. J. B. Phillips once wrote that we Christians have too small a concept of God.

We must learn to rebel against Satan's evil plans to derail the Kingdom of God. Satan is a liar and seeks to persuade Christians who are ignorant of the Bible's teaching to accept the world's point of view as truth. But we worship the God who is all loving and all powerful, and who hears and answers our prayers.

Chapter Thirteen

Your Labor Is Not in Vain
2 Kings 4:38-44; 6:1-7

 e long for and pray to see the mighty works of God restored in our generation. But there are times when we do not seem to be contributing to their restoration. We discover that we are not perfect. We have defects, often feel inadequate, make mistakes and suffer accidents. Yet God continues to work His loving and perfect will even in the midst of such unfortunate things. We will study three of Elisha's miracles that border on the magical. Some scholars dismiss such miracles as legends that were later built around these two famous prophets. But they are all true, they actually happened; and they are beautiful testimonies of the truth that God can cover all our defects as we serve Him.

Professor Ronald S. Wallace once remarked, "Our labor may seem to be in vain. It may seem to become spoilt by mistakes, shortcomings and accidents. But it is not in vain. God is in control."[17] Even the Suffering Servant, whom the prophet Isaiah introduces in his prophecies about Jesus Christ, had times when he wondered if all was in vain. *"I have labored in vain; I have spent my* strength for nothing and vanity; yet surely my right is with the Lord, and my recompense with my God." (Isaiah 49:4) Jesus of course knew that His work was not in vain, but in saying this He identified with God's suffering servants everywhere who have feelings that all they do is in vain.

Miracles are given by God as signs that point to His truth. Paul expresses the basic truth of these three miracles best, when he describes the ministry of a person who ministers in the resurrection power of Jesus Christ: *"Therefore, my beloved brothers, be steadfast, immovable, always abounding in the work of the Lord, knowing that in the Lord your labor is not in vain."* (1 Corinthians 15:58) Paul said this immediately after his dynamic teaching about the power of the resurrection of Jesus Christ. It is Christ's resurrection that gives meaning to all work, *even when we make mistakes.* Later, Paul added these words, *"And let us not grow weary of doing good, for in due season we will reap, if we do not give up."* (Galatians 6:9)

Christ and our mistakes

There was a famine in the land during Elisha's time of ministry, and he told one of the "sons of the prophets" to prepare a stew out of herbs. The young man was eager to serve God but made a mistake. He was full of zeal but had no knowledge of which plants were edible. He saw a plant that looked like a wild gourd. Perhaps he was from a different region where they could find good, edible wild gourds. But the ones he picked were poisonous! He made a nearly tragic mistake. But Elisha threw some flour into the pot, and the poison was removed.

Elisha, by the power of God, was able to purge the poison from the pot of stew. In so doing he covered over the mistakes of this overly zealous young prophet. Elisha was a powerful prophet who experienced amazing miracles, but he also was a wise leader who cared for his people and made allowances for them when they made mistakes. In this He was a foreshadowing of Christ, who in His unconditional love and unlimited power covered over the mistakes His own disciples made and who continues to use us today even when we fail.

The people of a certain Samaritan village once refused to welcome Jesus. Jesus' disciples wanted Jesus to command fire to come down from heaven and annihilate them, as Elisha had foolishly done in the beginning of his ministry. Jesus told them that an evil spirit from Satan was controlling their thoughts. Another incident happened in the Garden of Gethsemane, when Peter cut off the ear of a soldier with his sword. Jesus reprimanded him and put the ear back in place. Jesus knew the danger of power without compassion. Misguided zeal can bring great harm rather than good to the people we serve.

God allows His people to make mistakes. Unfortunately, many self-righteous leaders will not tolerate anyone in their communities who makes a mistake, even though they themselves are far from perfect. We seek to build perfect communities, failing to realize the truth of Dietrich Bonhoeffer's statement that those who look for a perfect community can never find it because it does not exist.

Who has not made mistakes? We make mistakes daily in the words we speak to one another, in our failure to maintain open and loving communication. Elisha was there to cover the mistakes of his disciples. And Jesus is here today to lead His disciples and to cover over the mistakes that we make.

Christ and our inadequacies

During the time of famine a farmer from a neigh-boring district brought a gift of food from the first fruits of his harvest to the community of the prophets. He himself was suffering, so his gift was a great sacrifice to him. He brought twenty loaves of barley and some fresh corn. Imagine the excitement of the young prophets when they saw the food.

The reaction of Gehazi, Elisha's servant, was just the opposite. He asked with sarcasm, "What, am I supposed to feed one hundred men with this little food?" Gehazi is a man we must watch carefully as we continue to study about the prophet Elisha. Even though he had the privilege of ministering with one of the great prophets of Israel, Gehazi's heart was selfish and greedy.

But Elisha spoke the Word of the Lord. *"Thus says the Lord, 'They shall eat and have some left over.'"* The miracle happened! All one hundred students ate, and there was food left over.

Four elements were present to make this miracle possible. First was the man's sincere offering of all that he had. Second was the Word of the Lord. Third was Elisha's total faith in that Word. Finally, there was Elisha's willingness to act on that Word *even when it appeared to be ridiculous.* These same elements make it possible to see miracles today. Some years ago a Swiss chef participated in our ministry in Korea. During the summer, large teams of Christians would go to Haeundae Beach in the city of Pusan to witness to the million people who visited the beach each day. No one who experienced the miracle will ever forget how this chef fed delicious chicken soup to more than two hundred hungry disciples, *using only one chicken! "For if the readiness is there, it is acceptable according to what a person has, not according to what he does not have."* (2 Corinthians 8:12)

The farmer's gift of loaves and corn were inadequate; the Swiss chef's one chicken was insufficient. But are not all of our efforts woefully inadequate? Yet precisely at those moments when our powers fail through our inadequacy, Jesus Christ is there to save the situation from failure and ourselves from disgrace. He only requires faith in action.

We are the fragrance of the knowledge of Christ. Our lives must spread the aroma of Christ to the world. But *"who is sufficient for these things?"* asks the Apostle Paul. (2 Corinthians 2:16) He answers his own question. *"Not that we are sufficient in ourselves to claim anything as coming from us, but our sufficiency is from God."* (2 Corinthians 3:5)

Sometimes it is easier to deal with our problems of material inadequacy than with our problem of spiritual inadequacy. Who is adequate to become an ambassador of reconciliation for Jesus Christ? Who is adequate to bring change to a nation that is in rebellion against God? The answer is, we must deal with our problem the same way the disciples of Jesus dealt with theirs. We must confess our helplessness and our lack of strength. We must respond to Jesus' offer to baptize us with His Holy Spirit. We must obey Jesus, who told His disciples to *"stay in the city until you are clothed with power from on high."* (Luke 24:49) *"If you then, who are evil, know how to give good gifts to your children, how much more will the heavenly Father give the Holy Spirit to those who ask Him!"* (Luke 11:13)

Christ and accidents

Mistakes can be corrected, and inadequacies can be filled. But what about accidents that happen, that threaten to undo all we are doing for the Kingdom of God?

Elisha's young prophets felt cramped in their small living space and desired to build a larger place. Elisha agreed, and they collected the materials and chose a site by the banks of the Jordan River. Then tragedy happened. One of the young men had borrowed a very expensive ax from a neighbor. As he was felling a log, his axhead fell into the water and sank to the bottom. Elisha cut off a stick and threw it into the water, and the iron axhead floated to the top and was easy to retrieve.

Accidents or other interferences happen often in Christian work. We are the "building of the Lord," and Satan wants to block us in every way. Things beyond our control, such as sickness, persecution, accidents or other events that threaten to stop the work of the Lord happen everywhere. Crises occur wherever men and women serve the Lord.

Nothing is outside the control of God

But the message of Elisha is that God can overcome all things that threaten to block what we are doing for the Lord. God will allow no accident or persecution to stop the work of His Kingdom. Paul wrote to the Thessalonian Christians that he would have visited them earlier, but that Satan hindered him. He also spoke of his "thorn in the flesh," which he called a "messenger of Satan" to block his work. But it did not stop his ministry. A young missionary lost an arm in an accident in Tanzania, and it caused great pain and suffering and even disappointment. But it did not stop the work she began. Today she leads an effective intercession ministry that changes nations. *Nothing is* outside the control of God!

Joseph suffered for thirteen years because of the rejection and sin of his family. But he later confessed to his brothers when they visited Egypt, *"It was not you who sent me here, but God. He has made me a father to Pharaoh, and lord of all his house and ruler over all the land of Egypt."* (Genesis 45:8)

Let us look back over our lives and see the accidents that have happened that threatened to stop the work of God's Kingdom. Yet God's Kingdom continued to advance. We have experienced God in His wisdom *laying His plans over the top of Satan's plans, to make them void.* He has removed the poison from the stew.

As Ronald S. Wallace used to say, "God can change poison into sweetness. He can multiply our small, insufficient offerings into abundance. He can make the axheads float."[18]

Questions for Further Thought and Discussions
Please read 2 Kings 4:38-44 and 6:1-7
before answering these questions.

1. How do you deal with your inadequacies? Are you able to acknowledge them and use them as the platform for God to work through you in an even greater way? Or do you feel that you must somehow "become more adequate" before God can use you? Read through Paul's Second Letter to the Corinthians again, thinking about God's solution for our inadequacies.

2. Are you tolerant of your own mistakes? How can we find the right balance between refusing to acknowledge our mistakes with a defensive attitude, and simply wishing to give up because we make so many mistakes? Ask God what He thinks about the mistakes you make as you minister to Him and others.

3. When you examine the community of which you are a part, do you find that you are tolerant of other people's mistakes, or are you judgmental when others make mistakes? What is the proper biblical approach to deal with mistakes in a community?

Notes

From Brokenness to Community

   From Brokenness to Community is the title of a small book written by Jean Vanier, based on lectures he gave at Harvard University. He speaks of broken people who give life to Christian community. "My experience has shown," he says, "that when we welcome people from this world of anguish, brokenness and depression, and when they gradually discover that they are wanted and loved as they are and that they have a place, then we witness a real transformation—I would even say *resurrection.*"[20]

   Vanier is the founder of the L'Arche communities, which are Christian communities for wounded people, with mental disabilities or mental illness, and for the people called to live with them. His teaching also includes the weaknesses, mistakes and inadequacies of those who are not mentally disabled.

   He teaches that we all are wounded; we all are poor and make mistakes. But we all are the beloved people of

God. Vanier emphasizes that Jesus *is* that broken person, that person we meet who feels inadequate or who makes mistakes. When we welcome one another in spite of our mistakes, or accidents or inadequacies, we are actually welcoming Christ in our midst. He says that one person, all alone, can never heal another person. People who are weak or broken must be brought into a loving community where healing can take place.

For this reason, according to Vanier, true Christian community is both a place of blessing and a place of pain. Why a place of pain? Because of conflict within each of us, conflict between the values of the world and the values of our community. There is the conflict of caring only for oneself, or of caring for one another. Community means to care for one another. Another conflict is the conflict between living independently or sharing our lives with one another in mutual acceptance.

At the heart of community is forgiveness, which unlocks the treasure chest of resources the Holy Spirit makes available for us to grow into the likeness of Jesus Christ. "We feel small and weak," says Vanier, "but we are gathered together to signify the power of God who transforms death into life."[21] We are then empowered to minister wholeness to a broken world.

Chapter Fourteen

Where Is Your Heart?
2 Kings 5:1-27

॰ ❦ ॰

*G*od is interested in our hearts, not just our talents or knowledge. He is seeking those who will love and worship Him in Spirit and in truth, and who will complete their worship by offering to Him their bodies as a living sacrifice. God spoke the following words to me many years ago. Perhaps He is speaking them now to you.

> *Give Me your heart, My son,*
> *And let your eyes delight in My way.*
> *I am not weary in waiting for you,*
> *My mercy falls as the new morning dew.*
> *Give me your heart, My son,*
> *And let your eyes delight in My way.*

The key question then for every disciple of the Lord is, "Where is your heart?" We may be busy with the affairs of the world in business or in politics, yet our hearts can be in God and not in the world. Or we can be busy in our local churches or mission societies and yet have our hearts set on worldly things; our hearts can be in the world. Jesus said, *"For where your treasure is, there your heart will be also."* (Matthew 6:21)

We will examine four people's hearts in this study. *Elisha* was an Israelite whose heart was in Israel. His heart was centered in God, and his life revealed the fruit of that intimate relationship. The heart of his servant *Gehazi*, however, was in the world. He longed for the things of the world rather than for God. He was never content in God alone. *Naaman* was a Syrian, and he lived a very busy life in the world as commander of the army of the king of Syria, but his heart was in Israel, that is, in the Lord. The fourth person was a *little slave girl.* She had been captured by the Syrian army and forced to work as a slave in Naaman's household. Yet she loved the Lord, and she loved her captors. Her heart was in God.

Elisha the man of God

We have seen the heart of Elisha through our previous studies. He served the Lord wholeheartedly. He had only one goal, that of glorifying God in all that he did. He was grounded in the Word of God and lived by that Word. He lived a life of an ongoing "conversation with God." He was a true servant of the Lord, totally available to Him at all times.

Naaman the commander of the Syrian army

Syria was one of the most important countries in the world; it was wealthy, highly cultured and beautiful. Its two great rivers, the Abana and the Pharpar, flowed from their source in the mountains of Lebanon, creating a beautiful oasis in the lush countryside around Damascus. Damascus was called the "White Pearl."

Naaman was the commander of the Syrian army. He was a very important man who enjoyed the best life that Syria could offer. He had ready access to the king and enjoyed his high position. He was a highly respected and valiant warrior. But *he was a leper.*

His life could be seen as a parable of the true man of the world who has everything but at the same time is hopelessly defiled. His disease was incurable. When it was discovered that Naaman had leprosy, all the wealth and culture of Syria lost its value to him. His position offered him everything, but it could not heal him.

We must understand Naaman's healing as a *holistic* healing. He was healed in his spirit and mind as well as in his body. He was "born again" and came to believe in the one true God. His nation had given up on him, but God had not. God healed him of his physical leprosy and restored him to perfect health. He also healed him of his *spiritual leprosy.* He delivered him from sin, from sickness and from Satan's control.

The little slave girl

Naaman became a seeker, but little did he realize that the person who would start him on the true journey to life was the little slave girl who served his wife. Just as God had placed Joseph in Egypt to save that nation, so God also placed this little Jewish girl in Syria to bring salvation to a key leader of that nation. God, in His sovereignty, laid His plans over the evil plans of Satan to enslave this little girl and placed her in Naaman's home to be His witness.

The history of Christian missions abounds in stories of slaves, especially women and small children, whose testimonies of their faith under oppressive circumstances resulted in salvation for whole nations. One of the best examples was that of the Vikings, many of whom were converted because of the living witness of captive women and children who lived among them. We must never underestimate the value and power of *Christian presence!* This little slave girl was an Israelite whose heart was in Israel, who loved God so much that she joyfully accepted her tragic situation and turned it into a testimony for the Lord. She not only had compassion for her master, she also had more knowledge about the solution to Naaman's problem than all the wise men, doctors or priests of Syria! We are reminded of the New Testament Christians who were scattered because of the great persecution of the church in Jerusalem, and who used their dispersion as an opportunity to witness to the Gospel of Jesus Christ. (Acts 8:1-4) Their witness resulted in the founding of the Antioch church, which became the first New Testament church to engage in cross-cultural missions!

Naaman's road to healing

There were five steps in Naaman's healing:

First, Naaman had to humble himself to listen to the wisdom of a child rather than to the wise men of Syria. Her advice was simple but persuasive. *"Would that my lord were with the prophet who is in Samaria! He would cure him of his leprosy."* (2 Kings 5:3) Jesus must have been thinking of this little girl when He prayed, *"I thank you, Father, Lord of heaven and earth, that you have hidden these things from the wise and understanding and revealed them to little children; yes, Father, for such was your gracious will."* (Matthew 11:25-26)

Second, Naaman had to give up his faith in the superiority of his own culture and in his own wealth and importance. He went to Israel full of pride and loaded down with gifts. He wanted to pay for his healing. He took letters from the king of Syria and rode in his best chariot with majestic horses in an attempt to impress Elisha. He thought he would gain immediate access to the most holy and revered prophet of Israel. He angrily said, *"Behold, I thought that he would surely come out to me and stand and call upon the name of the Lord his God, and wave his hand over the place and cure the leper."* (2 Kings 5:11) But Elisha would not even come out to meet Naaman. He ignored him.

Why did Elisha not rush out to meet Naaman? Because he was listening to God to know exactly what to do. Many people, seeking to serve the Lord with their zeal, react impulsively because of the urgency of the situation. Not so Elijah! He was not driven by the "tyranny of the urgent." Rather, he continued to listen to God in order to obey Him. Elisha was a wise leader, and he knew what he was doing. He also knew what Naaman needed. So another reason Elisha did not immediately go out to welcome Naaman was to allow God to work in Naaman's heart to prepare him for healing.

Third, Naaman had to be willing to go and wash himself in the Jordan River seven times. Naaman was learning *humility* through an ever-deepening experience of *humiliation.* He was greatly offended by Elisha's command. The Jordan River was muddy and dirty, not like the majestic rivers of his homeland. But he had no choice.

Every twelve years, there is a great festival at the Ganges River in India. In 2001, more than sixty-five million people went to wash away their sins in the Ganges. Legend has it that thousands of years ago, two gods were fighting and spilled four drops of nectar into the Ganges River. This resulted in healing waters for the world. This is a good symbol of all the world has to offer for the salvation of mankind.

All God offers is the life-giving blood of Jesus Christ, spilled out of His broken body for the salvation of the world. Naaman was offended at Elisha's command. Today likewise people are offended by the simplicity of the command to be washed in the blood of the Lamb for the forgiveness of sins.

Fourth, Naaman had to depend on the wisdom of his servants. They persuaded him by reminding him of the great word that Elisha had spoken to him. If he would only wash in the Jordan he would be cleaned from his leprosy! Naaman had finally come to the point of deep humility. He obeyed. *"And his flesh was restored like the flesh of a little child, and he was clean."* (2 Kings 5:14)

Fifth, Naaman had to return to Syria and live as a man of God in a pagan society. This would complete his healing. Naaman was saved and healed, in body and soul. We have met Naaman the commander of the army of Syria; then we met Naaman the leper, and Naaman the seeker. Now we meet Naaman the believer!

Naaman became a Syrian whose heart was in Israel. He remained a man of the world, but his heart was in God. He had to return and live in Syria to assume his same duties as before, but he would never go back and worship the false god Rimmon again. His heart now belonged to God, and he would worship God alone.

Elisha refused Naaman's offer of a gift, so Naaman asked instead for two mules' loads of earth to take back to Syria in order to build an altar on which he could worship and offer sacrifices to God. He asked for forgiveness for the times he would have to escort the king of Syria to the house of the god Rimmon to worship. Elisha knew his heart and gave him permission.

Gehazi the servant of Elisha

Gehazi should have been proud of his master, Elisha, for refusing to accept a gift for his ministry to Naaman. Instead, he thought Elisha was too spiritual and perhaps foolish. Gehazi's line continued all the way to Judas Iscariot and continues today.

Gehazi served in a holy position. But his heart was in the riches of the world. Rather than running toward God, as Elisha had taught him, he ran after Naaman's chariot to ask for a gift of money and clothes. This was not a sudden decision. For years, Gehazi's heart had been more in the world than in God. His heart was just now beginning to surface.

But Gehazi "went in and stood before his master." And the leprosy that had been on Naaman was now on Gehazi! Naaman, the "man of the world," was saved from the leprosy of Syria. Gehazi, the "man of the Church," was smitten with the leprosy of Syria! The leprosy of the world sometimes clings to the Church.

God does not judge His people by where our job is, or how we find entertainment. He does not judge us by our mistakes or failures. He judges us by where our heart is. But whether it be the leprosy of Naaman or the leprosy of Gehazi, we thank God that there is a River where we can wash and be made clean.

Questions for Further Thought and Discussion
Please read 2 Kings 5:1-27
before answering these questions.

1. Review the stages of Naaman's healing. The stages of Naaman's healing were also steps to his salvation. Remember that the New Testament uses the same word for "healing" and "salvation." Consider how you would use this approach to present the steps to salvation to a non-believer.

2. Consider again the four key people in this drama of Naaman's healing: Elisha, Naaman, the little slave girl, and Gehazi, the servant of Elisha. Of these four people, with whom would you identify?

3. We have said that the "leprosy of the world" sometimes clings to the Church. Consider not just your local church but the whole Church worldwide. Do you see evidences of this among Christian leaders, or in Christian communities or organizations? What is the solution?

Notes

Formation of the Heart

The word *heart* in Christian thinking refers not only to the emotional, sentimental feelings that often come to mind when one considers the word. The heart does include our emotions, but it also includes our intellectual thinking and reasoning. The heart is the seat of the will, and with our heart we make plans and set direction for our lives. Our hearts determine our character and our personality, so we are told in Scripture that we must guard our hearts.

Satan attacks our hearts and seeks to plant seeds of doubt, fear, anger, self-centeredness, rebellion against God and resentment against others in our community. This means that the heart can lead us either to God or away from His presence. We have seen the hearts of the four people in our present study. Now we must examine our own hearts.

Many writers on spirituality speak of *descending into the heart,* or of taking an *inward journey into the heart.* The purpose is to understand who we are and to begin the process of renewing our hearts. The first step is to ask the Holy Spirit to search our hearts and see if there be any wicked or grievous way in us; then we ask Him to lead us in the way everlasting. (Psalm 139:23-24) We must become aware of why we think and act the way we do, why we act selfishly in our relations with others in our community.

Spiritual transformation of the heart takes place in the Word and in prayer. I remember being taught by a godly professor in theological school that we should read the Bible on our knees, receiving the Word of God as His word speaking to us, and then responding in faith to the Holy Spirit who is seeking to form Christ within us. We must not *use the Bible* to learn information only, even if the information is about God; rather in it we must seek God's presence and His will. Then the Word of God, which is *"living and active, sharper than any two-edged sword, piercing to the division of soul and of spirit, of joints and of marrow, and discerning the thoughts and intentions of the heart"* (Hebrews 4:12) will change us radically. We have the example of the saints, such as St. Augustine, whose life changed totally when he read the Bible prayerfully and received the Word that the Spirit was implanting within him as he meditated and met God. God is faithful, and He will change our hearts when we surrender them to Him in adoration and devotion.

Chapter Fifteen

The Day of Salvation
2 Kings 6:24 -7:20

𒀸

*W*e come now to the question of why the Church of Jesus Christ exists. Jesus founded His Church to extend His Kingdom throughout the world. The clear reason the Church exists is to evangelize the nations, so that all people everywhere may have the opportunity to respond by faith to Jesus Christ's command to follow Him. *"I am the way, and the truth, and the life. No one comes to the Father except through Me."* (John 14:6) Emil Brunner best described the Church's mission by saying: "The Church exists by mission, as fire exists by burning!" [21]

God uses everyone who is committed to achieving His great purpose of bringing salvation to the world. In the midst of a national crisis of Israel, God found four willing men.

The siege of Samaria

Tension had continued to increase between Syria (Aram) and Israel. Syria's siege of Samaria resulted in famine so severe that people reverted to cannibalism. The cost of food rose sharply, driven by ungodly people who actually made a profit because of the siege. This was not unlike what we see today throughout the world, in individuals who make money off war or corporations that profit from world famine. Some governments actually are able to retain their power over the people by allowing famine to happen when they could prevent it.

When Israel's king heard the reports of cannibalism, he tore his clothes, put on sackcloth and mourned his people's fate. He suffered with his people. But he misplaced the blame by placing it on Elisha rather than on his own leadership. Elisha had healed Naaman, Syria's commander in chief, but now Syria was laying siege to Samaria. The king wondered whose side Elisha was on. Actually, Elisha represented God, and the problem was that the king was angry with God.

Elisha prophesied that the famine would end the next day. Elisha had a "conversational relationship" with God and knew how to listen to Him. But the royal officer who escorted the king cried out, *"If the Lord himself should make windows in heaven, could this thing be?"* (2 Kings 7:2) The king's officer mocked God! Elisha gave another prophecy, to the effect that the officer would see the end of the famine but would not be able to experience its fruits.

Four lepers

God kept His promise. The next day He caused the army of the Syrians to hear a great sound of chariots and horses, like a great army coming upon them. They panicked and fled, abandoning all their belongings.

Into this scene of hopelessness and seeming despair God sent four men. They were lepers who had been sitting begging at the entrance of the gate of Samaria. They concluded that whether they remained sitting where they were or whether they entered the city, they would die. So they decided to go to the camp of the Syrians. They had nothing to lose. When they entered the Syrians' camp they found it had been deserted. They found riches beyond their wildest dreams!

A truly amazing thing happened! The first people to enjoy the salvation of the Lord were four poor outcast beggars! D.T. Niles was right when he defined evangelism as *one beggar telling another beggar where to get rice!* God's salvation does not appear first to the powerful and the rich. Poor shepherds were the first to witness the birth of Jesus. Throughout His ministry, Jesus placed more emphasis on the poor, the rejected and those despised, saying that they would be first to enter the Kingdom of God! The Pharisees, the Sadducees and scribes, along with the more influential members of Israel's society, turned their backs on Jesus. The poor welcomed Him.

In the beginning, the four lepers enjoyed all their newly found riches and hid everything. But then new revelation dawned on them, and they said to one another: *"We are not doing right. This day is a day of good news. . . . Let us go and tell the king's household."* (2 Kings 7:9) On the one hand, they acted out of fear of punishment, but on the other hand, *they were the bearers of good news!* They had a message so powerful that they could tell it to the king! After all, they were better off than the king. He was starving, and they were rich. Four miserable lepers, total outcasts without any human hope, despised by everyone who saw them! Yet they were better off than the king. Why? Because they had the good news!

Heralds of good news

Heralds of good news! The message of salvation that even kings and world leaders long to hear! An urgent message that must be proclaimed to the whole world *now*, before it is too late! We must not keep silent. *"If we are silent and wait until the morning light, punishment will overtake us."* (2 Kings 7:9) Paul would later add, *"Woe to me if I do not preach the Gospel!"* (1 Corinthians 9:16)

This is the mission of the Church; there is no greater calling. We are no better than those four lepers. We, like them, are just beggars who have found spiritual food and now can tell the whole world where to find it. The lepers did absolutely nothing to gain this new life. And that is the way it is with each one of us. *"By grace you have been saved through faith. And this is not your own doing; it is the gift of God, not a result of works, so that no one may boast."* (Ephesians 2:8-9)

But in seeking to understand all that God is saying to us through this story of the four lepers, we must remember that they discovered physical food, not just spiritual food. We have learned that Naaman was healed spiritually and so became a true believer in God, but also that he was cleansed of his physical disease of leprosy. Healing is holistic, for the spirit, soul and body. Salvation is for the whole person, not just for the soul. Hundreds of millions of people live today in severe poverty; some face imminent starvation. Yet leading world economists tell us that poverty can be eradicated if nations that are developed will share with the underdeveloped nations. Who will take the leadership in sharing the world's resources and wealth? God's *family* must take the lead! Christians, those who are committed to Jesus Christ and His Word, are the ones called by God to solve the hunger problem in the world today. *"Is not this the fast that I choose . . . to share your bread with the hungry and bring the homeless poor into your house; when you see the naked, to cover him? If you pour yourself out for the hungry and satisfy the desire of the afflicted, then shall your light rise in the darkness."* (Isaiah 58:6, 7, 10) The last request the elders of the Jerusalem Church made to Paul and Barnabas before these two apostles set out on their great missionary journeys was to remember the poor. Paul replied that he was very eager to do so. We are called to proclaim the Gospel to the world, to announce the Good News of eternal life in Jesus Christ, to free those who are in prison and to satisfy the needs of those who are hungry and outcast from society.

The cross of salvation

An element of judgment is always present when the Gospel of Jesus Christ is proclaimed. It brings life to those who welcome it but death to those who reject Jesus. Judgment always comes to those who choose death. God does not predestine a person to eternal death. Each person must choose between life and death. On that amazing day when the four men proclaimed the salvation of God, only one man was judged: the king's royal officer who had mocked the Word of God! All the people trampled on him as they rushed to plunder the wealth that had been abandoned by the fleeing Syrian army. The women who practiced cannibalism were not judged. God understood their misery and the desperate situation of their starvation. But they did not mock God.

The danger remains today of laughing at the message of the cross of Christ. Today the cross remains a stumbling block to those who reject God's way of salvation. But the good news is that the cross remains today as the power of God and the wisdom of God to those of every nation who will accept Jesus as Lord.

Questions for Further Thought and Discussion
Please read 2 Kings 6:24-7:20
before answering these questions.

1. Do you think God had a purpose in revealing the source of salvation for His people of Israel during the national crisis to four lepers? If so, what would His purpose be? Remember that God had already healed a leper from Syria. (2 Kings 5)

2. Do you agree with the theologian Emil Brunner who said, "The Church exists by mission, as fire exists by burning"? Do you agree that the Church's chief reason for existing is to proclaim the Gospel to all nations? Give your reasons for believing this.

3. The Bible says that salvation is holistic; God cares not only for our souls eternally but also for our bodies and for the quality of life lived here on earth. The majority of the world's people live in poverty, with some nations experiencing famine and starvation due to lack of access to food. What must we as Christians do to alleviate world hunger? What are some steps of mercy we must take? What are some steps of justice we must take?

Notes

The Evangelization of the World

Jesus said, *"This gospel of the kingdom will be proclaimed throughout the whole world as a testimony to all nations, and then the end will come."* (Matthew 24:14) The task remains today, and it is the central task of the Church. Samuel Zwemer was known as the great apostle to the Muslims. He once remarked that "the unoccupied fields of the world await those who are willing to be lonely for the sake of Christ."[22] He was perhaps the first person to exhort Christians to "make a life, not a living." Throughout the history of the Church, thousands of young men and women have answered the command of Christ to preach the Gospel to all creation and make disciples of all nations.

John R. Mott, one of the leaders of the Student Volunteer Movement and the YMCA, which was a highly evangelistic movement in his day, spoke the following words in the early 1900s. He may have spoken them for today.

> *Our Saviour said, "I must work the works of Him that sent me, while it is day: the night cometh, when no man can work." Therefore, friends, in view of the awful need of men who tonight are living without Christ; in view of the infinite possibilities of the life related to Christ as mighty Saviour and risen Lord; in view of the magnitude of the task which confronts the Church of this generation; in view of the impending crisis and the urgency of the situation; in view of the conditions which favor a great onward movement with the Church of God; in view of the dangers of anything less than a great onward movement; in view of the great cloud of witnesses who gather around us, of those who subdued king-*

doms and wrought righteousness—yes, in view of the constraining memories of the Cross of Christ and the love wherewith He hath loved us, let us rise and resolve, at whatever cost of self-denial, that live or die, we shall live or die for the evangelization of the world in our day.[23]

Chapter Sixteen

Finishing the Task
2 Kings 13:14-25

𐰼

*W*e come to the end of an era of two of the greatest prophets of Israel. Elijah and Elisha had walked with God through the land of Israel for many years. Just as Moses had Joshua to continue his ministry, so Elijah had Elisha. Following in the footsteps of his predecessor Elijah, Elisha had brought life where there was only death. He also, like Elijah, offered salvation to foreigners as well as Jews: Elijah to the widow of Zarephath (1 Kings 17) and Elisha to Naaman (2 Kings 5). Elisha asked Elijah for a double portion of God's Spirit who rested on him, and then proceeded to work many more miracles than Elijah.

Elisha points to the future ministry of Jesus. The New Testament mentions Elisha only one time, but Jesus is the one who mentioned him and He did so in the very beginning of His ministry. In Luke 4:27, Jesus referred to the healing of Naaman the Syrian. Jesus made it very clear from the beginning that His salvation was for the whole world and not only for the Jewish people. He referred to both Elijah and Elisha as prophets who reached out to non-Jewish people to offer healing and salvation. These two prophets stood between Abraham, who received the covenant from God that promised salvation to all humankind, and Jesus, who came to offer salvation to the whole world. The names "Elisha" and "Jesus" have basically the same meaning: *God saves.* Elisha was a shadow, albeit dimly seen with many imperfections, of God's salvation in Jesus Christ.

Now Elisha lay dying, and Israel faced a darker future in which they would have to fight their enemies without their strong deliverer. King Joash faced a crisis that would affect his future, and he *wept before Elisha.* But his weeping was not for Elisha or for his nation; he wept for himself. He considered Elisha to be the strength of the nation; he could not envision a life without this man of God.

King Joash was not ready to stand up and be the man of God he was being called to become. He was complacent, satisfied with depending on another stronger man to continue doing what he himself should do. This story continues to speak even today to tell us again of God's plan for our lives. We are men and women, and children, of destiny; God has a great plan for each of our lives. He will use us without limitations when we answer His call and commit to following Him completely.

Our life is God's instrument for world evangelization

The king cried out, "My father, my father! The chariots of Israel and its horsemen!" The chariots and horsemen represented Israel's strong army that had been decimated by the Syrians. But Elisha knew that the real *chariots and horsemen of Israel* were not of flesh and blood. Earlier, when the king of Syria had surrounded the city of Dothan with a large army with many horses and chariots, Elisha's servant was greatly troubled and asked his master what they should do. Elisha's reply was, *"Do not be afraid, for those who are with us are more than those who are with them!"* Then Elisha prayed for God to open his servant's eyes. The servant looked, and *"behold, the mountain was full of horses and chariots of fire all around Elisha."* (2 Kings 6:11-17)

The two great apostles of our faith, the Apostle Paul and the Apostle John, identified both the enemy and the One who conquered the enemy. Paul said, *"For we do not wrestle against flesh and blood, but against the rulers, against the authorities, against the cosmic powers over this present darkness, against the spiritual forces of evil in the heavenly places."* (Ephesians 6:12) The Apostle John told us the confidence we have in Jesus Christ: *"Little children, you are from God and have overcome them, for he who is in you is greater than he who is in the world."* (1 John 4:4) Jesus sometimes sends His angel hosts with the "chariots of God" to fight on behalf of His people. But Jesus Himself is the victor. He is the one who has overcome Satan and all his forces of death and destruction. He is the Deliverer today.

> *My help, my deliverer, O Spirit of power;*
> *Joy of the helpless at this my dark hour;*
> *Thy thoughts revive my soul by day and by night,*
> *Great is the Lord above, my joy and my life.*
>
> David E. Ross
> May be sung to the tune of *Be Thou My Vision*

King Joash had witnessed the power of God upon Elisha that made him stronger than all of Israel's chariots and horsemen. He wept because he could not imagine living without this man's power of prayer and influence on the nation.

"Take a bow and arrows"

Elisha ignored the king's weeping. He was not interested in his tears of sorrow or his confession of weakness. Joash would soon come face to face with his enemies, and he had no time to shed tears or brood over his tragedies. That same power now had to reside in the king! Elisha knew he must prepare the king for action. So he told him to take up a bow and arrows. Then he told him to draw the bow.

Elisha told the king to open the window eastward toward his enemies and shoot the arrow. *"The Lord's arrow of victory!"* shouted Elisha. This is a faint foreshadowing of Jesus and His disciples after the resurrection. The disciples were scared, ridden with guilt and felt helpless. At the mountain when Jesus appeared to them, some of the disciples still doubted. But Jesus did not allow them to mourn over their losses and weaknesses. He ignored their problems totally and said, *"Go into all the world and proclaim the gospel to the whole creation."* (Mark 16:15) He commissioned them to evangelize the world!

A life totally committed to Jesus Christ, whom Jesus then sends into the world to be His witness, is God's greatest tool to make the nations believe. The most powerful weapon in spiritual warfare against Satan is a life filled with the Holy Spirit and lived to the glory of God without compromise.

Too many Christians are like King Joash. They sit around feeling inadequate, feeling unable to do anything significant for the Lord. They think that someday, if God were to "call" them, they would go out and do something for the Lord. But God has already called us, and His sending is inherent in His calling. *"You did not choose me, but I chose you and appointed you that you should go and bear fruit."* (John 15:16) God has already sent us into the world! When we know that we are in the world because God has sent us, then our lives will be a powerful witness to God wherever we go and through whatever we do. Our lives are like an arrow, straight, sharp, flying in only one direction. We must be single-minded in proclaiming the victory of the Lord.

"Elisha laid his hands on the king's hands"

The king was not alone. Elisha's anointing was upon him. This was the assurance of his victory. The psalmist, singing of God's love and care for His people, says, *"You hem me in, behind and before, and lay Your hand upon me."* (Psalm 139:5) When God calls us to follow Him and obey His will, He *places His hands over our hands,* giving us the anointing power and authority of His Holy Spirit for the task He has called us to perform. God's anointing is the presence of His Holy Spirit both in us and also upon us, to use us to the maximum for His glory. We no longer need to fear or worry; we can cast all our anxieties on Him, for He cares for us.

We are called to finish the task of world evangelization

We are not only called to let our lives be God's instrument to bless the world; we are also called to *finish the task* set before us. Elisha told the king to take the arrows and strike the ground with them. He struck three times and then stopped. Elisha was angry with him and told him he should have struck the ground five or six times, then he would have completely destroyed the Syrian forces. Elisha was saying that the king was not totally committed to destroying the enemies of God. He was not enthusiastic about the command Elisha had given him; he struck the ground in *form* but not in *substance.*

The danger remains of being self-centered and half-hearted in the ministry to which God has called us. God requires *wholeheartedness* in every area of our lives. God blessed Caleb throughout his life, even to a very old age, because Caleb followed the Lord wholeheartedly! (Joshua 14:8) How easy it is to become intellectually converted to a great idea and then not live it out in practice. How often the people of God become satisfied with partial obedience rather than complete obedience. Many are excited about changing the world, until obstacles come along that cause their vision to fade away.

Moses as a young man had been so filled with zeal to deliver his people from bondage in Egypt that he made mistakes and acted unwisely. He became disillusioned, lost his vision and settled down to a complacent life in Midian. But one day he saw a bush burning with a fire that was unquenchable. He met God again, and he knew that God was a God of fire.

We are members of the *Community of the Holy Fire*, the fire of the Holy Spirit who lives within us. The fire of God's Spirit is the fire of His love. He may cause us to go through trials of burning fire in order to equip us to complete our vision. But the fire of His Holy Spirit is always with us, loving us and empowering us to continue to the end with a whole heart.

The responsibility to finish the task is laid upon each one of us personally and individually. It is non-transferable and urgent. To finish the task of world evangelization will require radical obedience to Jesus Christ for life. And it will require the elimination of all things in our lives that hinder our running the race to completion.

We are promised the power of the Holy Spirit to complete the task

The last miracle that came from this great man of God, Elisha, was perhaps the most unusual. Elisha died and was buried in a tomb. Many tombs in those days were simply caves, or tombs carved out of soft rock. Perhaps this was the kind of tomb prepared for Elisha. The next spring, a band of marauding Moabites invaded Israel. A man was being buried, and when the people saw the Moabites advancing they quickly threw him into the tomb of Elisha. *"As soon as the man touched the bones of Elisha, he revived and stood on his feet."* (2 Kings 13:21)

The power of God was so great in Elisha that even after His death, God's Spirit continued to give life to the dead! It was not Elisha's spirit that caused the dead man to come back to life but rather the Holy Spirit of God. Elisha was the disciple of Elijah, whom the Apostle James describes as *"a man with a nature like ours."* But James continues: *"[Elijah] prayed fervently that it might not rain, and for three years and six months it did not rain on the earth. Then he prayed again, and heaven gave rain, and the earth bore its fruit."* (James 5:17-18)

Elisha had walked in close communion with the Spirit of God, and even after his death the Holy Spirit continued to work in power. This amazing miracle that God worked through His servant Elisha even after his death leads us directly into the New Testament. Jesus had promised His disciples that He would not leave them as orphans but rather would send His Holy Spirit to be in them and with them. One of the greatest Catholic writers, Francois Mauriac, said that as soon as the Apostles received the Holy Spirit at Pentecost, they manifested God so strikingly that all those who had murdered Christ must have believed that Christ had returned. He said, "When the tomb had been closed over His dead body, there was no doubt in their minds that the affair was finished. . . but now Jesus' presence was felt throughout the city."[24]

God is showing us through Elisha that this same power of His Holy Spirit is available to His Church today. The Spirit continued to work throughout the age of the Old Testament, but it was not until Pentecost that the promised Holy Spirit was poured out upon the whole Church. This power is available to every Christian today who responds to Jesus' invitation to baptize us with His Holy Spirit. The results are clear: *"But you will receive power when the Holy Spirit has come upon you, and you will be My witnesses in Jerusalem and in all Judea and Samaria, and to the end of the earth."* (Acts 1:8)

The modern world has yet to see the power of God's people who will take God seriously, as did Elijah and Elisha. When we respond to God with a life-long passion to become His instruments to bless the world, His Holy Spirit will light a fire in our hearts that can never be extinguished. Then God will use our lives, just as He used Elisha's life, not only during our lifetime but also to bless the generations to come.

Questions for Further Thought and Discussion
Please read 2 Kings 13:14-25
before answering these questions.

1. We have said that a life totally committed to Jesus Christ, whom Jesus then sends into the world to be His witness, is God's greatest tool for world evangelization. This is the life of the person who understands that true spirituality does not flow inward, deeper into one's self, but rather outward, as a river of life for the healing of the nations. Is your life flowing in this direction? If not, what can you do to cause the river of life within you to flow out to the world?

2. It is easy to be in intellectual agreement with the idea of needing to witness for Christ to the world, yet not live it out in practice. What will it require to finish the task of making disciples of all nations? What is God saying to you personally?

3. Consider all the things God has revealed to you during your study of Elijah and Elisha. Make note of some of the more important ones, then ask the Holy Spirit to strengthen your inner person to enable you to put these things into practice. Use the space below to write down your ideas.

Notes

Interpreting the Old Testament in Light of the New Testament

The task of each Christian is to proclaim the biblical witness to Jesus Christ. We have discovered through our study of Elijah and Elisha that there is a unity between the Old and New Testaments. Walter C. Kaiser has made a great contribution toward understanding the unity of the Old Testament and New Testament in reminding us that "the goal of the Old Testament was to see both Jews and Gentiles come to a saving knowledge of the Messiah who was to come." He points out that God's original plan is found in the opening chapters of Genesis, even earlier than His covenant with Abraham. "God's eternal plan was to provide salvation for all people; it was never intended to be reserved for one special group, such as the Jews, even as an initial offer!"[25]

Our hope is that through your study of these two great prophets—Elijah and Elisha—you will come to see that the Bible is one book, not two. The Old Testament prepares us for the New Testament. The promises of the Old Testament find their deeper meaning and fulfillment only in the New Testament.

May the Holy Spirit of knowledge, wisdom and insight enrich you as you continue to search for God's treasures in His *One Book,* the Bible. And may He empower you to bear fruit throughout the world as you obey His Word.

Bibliography

1. See Robin Mark's website at http://robinmark.com
2. Ronald S. Wallace, *Elijah and Elisha* (Edinburgh: Oliver and Boyd, 1957). This book is currently out of print and may be difficult to find. The reader may benefit by reading his later book, *Readings in 1 Kings* (Eugene, Oregon: WIPF and STOCK Publishers, 1995).
3. Ronald S. Wallace, from a lecture series given at Columbia Theological Seminary, March-May, 1972.
4. *Ibid.*
5. Thomas Merton, *Bread in the Wilderness* (New York: New Direction Publishing Company, 1953), pp. 87-94.
6. Wallace, *ibid.*
7. Notes from a lecture on Martin Buber by Ronald S. Wallace, Columbia Theological Seminary, March-May, 1972.
8. Ronald S. Wallace, *Readings in 1 Kings*, pp. 133-134.
9. Henri Nouwen, *The Inner Voice of Love* (New York: An Image Book by Doubleday, 1996), pp. 107-108.
10. Luis Bush, lecture at Northeast Asia Discipleship Training School, Kona, Hawaii, on March 16, 2012.
11. Gary Parrett and S. Steve Kang, *Teaching the Faith, Forming the Faithful* (Downers Grove, Ill.: InterVarsity Press, 2009).

12. Alexander Maclaren, *Expositions of the Holy Scripture, Vol. 2* (Grand Rapids, Mich.: Wm. B. Erdmans Publishing Co., 1942), pp. 846-848.

13. D.S. Cairns, *The Faith That Rebels* (London: Student Volunteer Movement, 1928), p. 247.

14. Notes from a lecture on Charles Spurgeon by Ronald S. Wallace, Columbia Theological Seminary, March-May, 1972.

15. Cairns, *ibid.*

16. Cairns, p. 209.

17. Wallace, *Elijah and Elisha*, pp. 125-126.

18. *Ibid.*

19. Jean Vanier, *From Brokenness to Community* (Mahwah, N.J.: Paulist Press, 1992), p. 15.

20. *Ibid*, p. 52.

21. Emil Brunner, *The Word and the World* (New York: C. Scribner's Sons, 1931), p. 108.

22. Samuel Zwemer, *The Glory of the Impossible,* Chapter 8 (London: Student Volunteer Movement, 1911), p. 215-231.

23. John R. Mott, *Missionary Issues of the Twentieth Century* (Nashville, Tenn.: Press of the Publishing House, M. E. Church, South, 1901), p. 23.

24. Francois Mauriac, *Magnificat* Devotional: *How Christ's Resurrection Conquers the World* (Yonkers, N.Y.: Magnificat Inc., 2012), May 21, 2012.

25. Walter C. Kaiser, *Mission in the Old Testament* (Grand Rapids, Mich.: Baker Books, 2000), p. 10.

CPSIA information can be obtained at www.ICGtesting.com
Printed in the USA
BVOW031805170613

323538BV00001B/4/P

9 781622 308057